Immigrants:
Unleashing the Economic Force at Our Door

by

OLIVER PURSCHE
with Dan England

TABLE OF CONTENTS:

FOREWORD

(and a quick look at the state of the debate about immigration):

I make my living by analyzing financial and economic data. Whether it is making sound decisions for clients as a Money Manager, or trying to bring perspective as a frequent guest on the major business programs internationally or writing for publications such as Forbes and the Wall Street Journal, I am forced to deal with economic reality and not social fantasy. That's why I have written this book.

The debate on immigration in America seems to be about everything except what it should be -- the economic health of this country. We need immigrants. Lots of them. We need to encourage them to come here, we need to make the path to citizenship smooth and we need to bolster their chances for success so they can pay taxes, strengthen entitlements such as Social Security and Medicare, and most importantly, build the financial base of our economy which is being eroded daily.

I am generally a financially, socially and politically conservative person. I move in circles where people pay a great deal of attention to financial matters. But I am frustrated when normally rational and well educated people come out with ideas that are counter-productive to their own prosperity and to that of the country. What you will read in this book is not social ideology or some "vision" of a "diverse population all working for the common good." I am interested in facts and policies that achieve viable economic ends. That's what this book is about.

As we consider this important matter, I hope we can at least agree on the facts everyone is, or should be, working with.

- There are approximately 8 million legal immigrants (about 5 percent of the workforce)

- There are an estimated 11.5 to 12 million illegal immigrants in the United States.

- As of the January 2013, there are approximately 14 million Americans out of work. Of those 14 million, roughly 6.5 million have been unemployed for more than six months and thus have dim prospects of finding a job in the near term.

- Only a relatively small portion of the work immigrants do is part of an underground economy of cash only, on which no taxes are paid.

- In many states, the children of illegal immigrants are part of school systems, as they should be because, as we will see, we need an increasingly educated work force.

- And at the same time, one of the greatest drags on the economy, health care costs, are extended to illegals through the hospital emergency system, which is hardly a health care plan and is one of the most expensive ways to treat anyone.

So given these realities, how do we fashion policies that make financial sense and effectively employ the human capital that immigrants represent? In short, how do we unleash the amazing economic force that is standing at our barely opened door wanting the chance to participate fully in this enterprise (and still experiment) we call America.

CHAPTER 1

The impact of Immigration: A long term view

I'm glad to see that our elected officials, on both sides of the aisle, have finally realized that immigration reform is absolutely necessary. So far, however, the proposals made by the U.S. Senate in early 2013 are still too narrow and do not address our financial problems enough. This book will illustrate the critical need for immigration reform, based on our short-term and long-term economic needs, not interest-group driven or short-sighted political motivations.

In my view, the United States needs to develop a deliberate and comprehensive immigration policy that can reshape our entire nation, and greatly improve our finances. By focusing on the economic benefits immigrants can bring to the United States, we can:

1. Strengthen and regain Americas economic and business dominance in the world

2. Reduce and eliminate our foreign debts and deficits to permanently balance our budget

3. Reverse the decline and restore the solvency of our Social Security, Medicare and Medicaid programs.

Few people in America today can be happy about the state of our immigration policy, or the myriad policies that rule the daily lives of immigrants – legal, and illegal. The current practices carry with them unsustainable costs: missed tax revenues and lost economic potential and growth. There is also the cost of underdeveloped human opportunity and the social impact of disrupted families. The current polarized nature of politics in this country is, of course, making things worse. Rhetoric by media personalities and public officials distort facts and falsely blame immigrants for either causing or adding to our unemployment woes. Fearful conservatives want high fences and punishing crackdowns. Unrealistic liberals campaign for open borders and costly services for illegal aliens. These positions are shouted, hailed and hardened. And we as a nation are getting nowhere on the issue at a time when tax revenues are down, the economy languishes, and unemployment remains high, while three and half million jobs go unfilled. We must address our economic needs, and in doing so need to be open minded about immigration.

In short, we need a deliberate, well-constructed set of policies that address our current and future needs – in the most economically advantageous manner possible.

Migration and immigration has been a part of the United States since the beginning of our history – just like it has for every other prosperous country down through the years. . Just as importantly, we need to understand that immigration is part of the solution to our economic difficulties, not the problem. As a registered Republican and fiscally conservative person, I have spent a great deal of time thinking about this issue. The "easy" statements are emotional and short-sighted – "kick'em out" and "let'em be" are neither practical nor constructive, as they do nothing to really help our economic situation. I have tried to put aside my pre-existing beliefs and biases in an effort to come up with a workable plan that serves America's best interest and helps us regain our competitive edge around the world, and address the impending doom that is our Social Security, Medicare and Medicaid systems. I have looked at what other countries have done, the mistakes they have made and the policy decisions they got right.

The United States is in a unique position right now. In spite of all the talk about unsustainable debt levels, the debt crisis in Europe and overall global growth slowdown has kept the United States in a relatively desirable fiscal position and has thereby given our politicians and financiers the ability to kick the can a little further down the road. This of course will do great harm to the next generations – our children, grandchildren and beyond. We must act now, to save the present and the future.

After much thought and research, I have come to believe that the current system can only be saved in one of two ways:

Either we pass laws that make the above mentioned social programs unavailable to anyone who has earned more than a certain sum over their lifetime, or has a net-worth over a certain amount (a solution I certainly do not endorse).

Or, we reengineer the entire system, including our tax system, social services, education, and immigration policies. All of these services need to be looked at in aggregate and that a broad based solution is necessary.

Some Major Points of Debate about Immigration

The discussion needs to be about immigration policy, not illegal immigrants. This distinction is both critical and necessary if we are going to make any progress on this issue. As with any national debate, people come to the issue with multiple assumptions and definitions. My aim is to bring clarity to aspects of the debate and suggest those pathways of thinking that will help us all to make the most progress.

There are many presuppositions that will lead a person to have a view on any of these matters. Some, for example, have a bent towards "fairness," that is, the idea that "ordinary" Americans whose families have long been a part citizens of the county, who have paid their taxes and their bills, who have worked hard for a stake in the American dream and who have many generations of presence in the U.S. should not be asked to accept newcomers. Others have a stricter interpretation of the law and find this view galling, especially if the newcomers are undocumented and require services that must be paid for by the established population. That is one prism to view the problem but in the end unhelpful – not to mention incomplete.

This is essentially the same complaint that has come up whenever a wave of immigration has taken place in this country by those who were already here. But the waves happened anyway and in fact made the country stronger by almost any measure, certainly economically. The poor, tired and wretched, yearning to be free turned out to be highly motivated people eager to become productive, active citizens in the experiment called America.

From a historical perspective, we should recognize that in fact "No one is from here. Even the earliest of settlers of this great land, the American Indians, crossed what is now known as the Bering Strait some 12,000 years ago. Later in history, "the natives" of course, had to contend with waves of European ships that came ashore – I suspect they were not big fans of immigration either.

In the past few decades, immigrants have played a key role in our economy. If it were not for immigration, some of our greatest public companies might not exist. Just look at the composition of the S&P 500 – of the 500 companies included in the index, 204 of them were started by immigrants or children of immigrants. Take for example, Sergey Brin who was born in Russia, he founded Google. Jerry Yang, who was raised in Taiwan founded Yahoo, while Andrew Grove, born and raised in Hungary started Intel. The discussion and debate needs to be about immigration, not illegal immigrants. Once it does, most will recognize that immigrants have always been prolific entrepreneurs and job creators, and that they will significantly add to the prosperity of the United States. This is true for a simple reason – only the bold and courageous are willing to leave everything they know and love behind for the chance of a better future. Given that opportunity, they will stop at nothing to try to make it.

Monthly Business Formation by Immigrants and U.S. Born

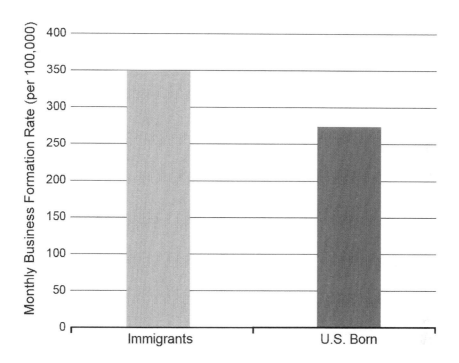

Source: Fairlie. R.W., "Estimating the Contribution of Immigrant Business Owners to the U.S. Economy," Small Business Administration, Office of Advocacy (Nov 2008)

Putting emotions and politics aside, my viewpoint and argument is an economic one. People do come to this country for a better life. Most of them not only want to be here to make more money than they can in their country of origin, but they actually want to participate in the enterprise of America. They want to put down roots. They want to buy houses. They want their kids to go to school here and learn English and have access to technology. If that means pulling up sweet potatoes for years on end, then so be it. But for their children, they want something better. This is the classic definition of the American Dream.

Immigrants are going to come no matter what. We can hound them and marginalize them, we can have them pursued by self-described vigilantes in all-their self-righteous splendor, and we can drive them underground. But they will still be here -- afraid of being separated from their kids, afraid that some agent will come calling, afraid that they will be deported -- yet all the while determined to seize a better life for themselves and their children. Remember, migration is a very natural phenomenon, one that always has and always will be driven by commerce and opportunity. Simply put, people will go to where there is an opportunity for a better life, no matter what the obstacles or risks. America and Americans should become very worried if we stop being the destination of choice for immigrants.

We need to embrace their desire, encourage the most hard working and intelligent of them and swiftly and reasonably move them into a position of legality that brings in tax revenue for the greater good of us all.

As we will see later, the economic impact of immigrants, in particular once they assimilate into our society, is very significant. Countries with deliberate and progressive immigration policies are able to capitalize from this talent pool, and are greatly aiding their economies. The United States is benefiting from immigration as well. In New York City, for example, nearly 40% of new businesses are started by immigrants or their children. These immigrants and the business they have started have created tens of thousands of jobs for Americans.

It is with a basic economic perspective that I approach the issues in the immigration debate. The irony of it all, as will unfold in chapter 2, is that no matter how you spin the politics, the economics are dictating that immigration is the best and perhaps only viable solution to our own financial salvation. But first, we need to look in some detail our current economic crisis, and the much bigger crisis that is looming. Based on our demographics, in particular the aging population, as well as several other uncontested factors, it is clear that America needs to revamp its entire system. We need to reexamine our spending commitments, as well as reshape our tax system. We must encourage entrepreneurship and need to significantly raise revenues. This can only be done in conjunction with a smart and constructive immigration policy.

The dangers of the current short-term view

As Michael Chertoff, Secretary of Homeland Security said in 2006, "When you try to fight economic reality, it is at best and expensive and very, very difficult process and almost doomed to failure." I take that as a starting point in the discussion of immigration.

Currently, both sides of the argument are taking a short-term view of our immigration policy. Politicians are in essence proposing "solutions" to placate voters, and pander to the worst of our fears, placing blame for our problems onto someone else, lacking the courage to act deliberately and considering every move in light of the next election. If we continue along the current path of inaction, our economic condition will continue to worsen – on our current course, the United States will look like Greece by 2021.

As of August 2012, the United States has over $16 trillion in debt. By 2020, our national debt will be approaching $25 trillion and by 2030, the United States will spend over $1 trillion per year on interest for this debt. By way of comparison, in 1970, the year I was born, the national debt was about $400 billion, roughly 38% of GDP. Today our debt stands at about 105% of GDP and, unless we act, it will climb to over 150% by 2030.

The reason I chose 2030 as an endpoint to my demographic and economic study is because in 2030, babies being born at the time this book is being written, in 2012, will be turning 18 years old and will be preparing to enter college. Based on the current rate of tuition inflation, the cost of attending a four year private college or university will be over $600,000, and the cost of attending a State school will near $300,000 for a 4 year degree. These numbers a real, they frighten me and probably frighten you as well. We must undertake every effort to strengthen our economy to avoid these looming disasters.

There are plenty of examples throughout history of countries that have taken a similar short-term view, and the outcome has always been the same – failure.

Take Japan for example. Japan's economy was once the envy of the world. Remember the 1980's when every business school in America was prompting students to learn Japanese? Today, Japan's economy is faltering – projected growth from the once venerable nation is less than 2% over the next 5 years, most likely for the next decade. So what happened? Among other factors, Japan has one of the strictest immigration laws in the world, with virtually no illegal immigrants. At the root of the problem – high levels of spending related to social services, a shrinking populations (currently at 127 million, but projected to shrink to 90 million by 2050). And, Japan has an aging population, with nearly 1 out of 4 of its citizens being over 65 years of age, making Japan the "oldest" country in the world. By 2040, the median age in Japan will be greater than that of Palm Springs. This is alarming to me, because the similarities to the United States are significant.

An aging population is destructive because it greatly reduces the active workforce. Without workers who are increasing productivity and helping grow a country's economy, the future is bleak.

In the 1990's, Japan was facing a severe labor shortage. As a result, Japan decided to allow ethnic Japanese living abroad (primarily Latin America) to move to Japan and be awarded permanent residence status (similar to our Green Card system). It was as close to immigration as Japan would ever allow. Over the coming decade, these ethnic Japanese, primarily from Brazil, filled manufacturing and other manual labor jobs. However, in the late 2000s, in part as a result of the global financial crisis, faced with high unemployment numbers, the government did an about face and began paying these immigrants to leave Japan – all under the belief that by vacating jobs held by immigrants, Japan's unemployment rate would fall as "natural" Japanese would take the jobs (just like some argue that if we kick out the illegals, Americans will fill the jobs). Four years later, the unemployment rate is still as high, and the economic outlook has worsened. Leaders in Japan have finally begun to recognize that its aging population requires lots of costly care, both medical and non-medical care. To address this shortfall in the workforce, Japan has overturned its old policies. The Japanese government has begun to invite in foreign workers – in particular in the nursing field. Japan has recognized that the shortage of qualified labor can only be filled by immigrants – at least in the short and intermediate term, until their own workforce is sufficiently skilled to fill these jobs. Even with the current policy shift, officials' project that by 2030 there will be a shortage of 900,000 qualified nurses in Japan. As a result of shortsighted immigration policies, an aging population, low birth rates, a strong sense of nationalism, Japan faces a humanitarian and fiscal crisis of huge proportions. Japan's closed society, along with the same demographic trends that exist in the United States, have put the country in a weak economic position and may ultimately cost its citizens trillions of dollars in added costs, when a more proactive approach could have changed the course of the economy.

Another example of immigration policy gone wrong is Europe. Unlike Japan, Europe has one of the highest rates of immigration in the world. The European Union is one of the most aggressive experiments in immigration in world history. As part of its charter, citizens of the 17 member states of the EU can freely move from one country to the other – that's about a half a billion people who can migrate to any European country within the union. Many predicted that masses of unemployed from the poorer nations like Greece, Spain or Poland would migrate to the wealthy nations like Germany or Holland. In spite of the well-known economic difficulties in southern Europe there has been little migration to the north. There are two key factors influencing this: First, northern European nations, in response to the economic crisis and calls for more bailouts of their southern neighbors, have become more nationalistic. This has meant that migrants are being shunned, isolated and are having a very difficult time assimilating. Second, the different languages complicate the assimilation process, and in light of the difficulties of assimilating into a new society, potential migrants are fighting the natural desire to remain "home." Absent conditions that foster immigration and migration, especially without economic incentive to move, the process becomes highly unpleasant. As a result, migration over the past decade has been minimal, with only three percent of the working population in Europe working in a country outside of their land of birth. I suspect that as the economies of southern Europe deteriorate, we may witness a greater level of migration – time will tell.

Both Europe and Japan made the same error. Both took an oversimplified approach to immigration which did not take into account economic needs and instead focused on ideals and politics. In Europe as in Japan, immigrants are being discriminated against and feel alienated, while the native population feels overwhelmed by all the changes immigration brings with it. The lesson I'm taking from this: Immigration without a clear economic policy doesn't work, neither does "banning" immigration.

Today, in part as a result of our own economic difficulties and high unemployment rate, and in part in reaction to our current policies, immigration from Mexico and other parts of South America is not just declining, but reversing. According to a 2012 study by the Pew Hispanic Center, "Mexican immigration may have actually reversed in 2011, with outflows surpassing immigration to the U.S. As former governor of Utah and former U.S. ambassador to China and Singapore John Huntsman recently wrote in a Wall Street Journal opinion piece, "future economic growth will depend in large part on our ability to maintain an edge in human capital". This means we must focus on immigration as a key economic driver rather than solely as a security issue. Immigration contributes to a healthier demographic profile – bringing younger workers to an aging population. Most important, immigrants add to America's competitive strength in a global economy.

Number of Patents Granted per 10,000
Post-College Graduates

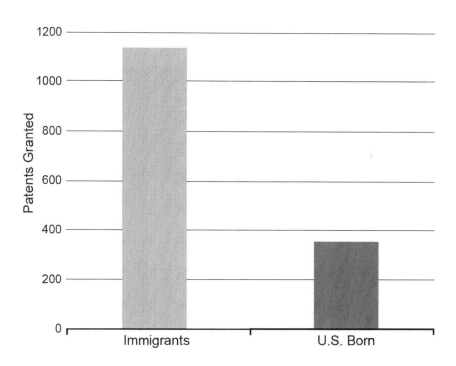

Source: Patents granted over the period 1998-2003. Hunt and Gauthier-Loiselle (2003),
Table 1

The benefits of taking a long-term approach

All nations in the world experience various forms of immigration
– some inbound, some outbound. There have been many different
approaches, in most cases the shortsighted and short-term solutions
have ended disastrously, with the "home" population inevitably growing restless and unhappy as their economies are negatively affected
by these policies. This is, of course, what is occurring in the United
States today. We are paying the price for bad decisions and poorly

thought out policies from past decades. Looking around the world, economic figures indicate that our neighbor to the north may have struck a balance that appears to be working best. That's right, Canada.

Canada is a country that has taken a proactive approach to immigration. Long standing in the shadow of the United States, Canadians now have a more formidable and prosperous economy than the United States. By any measure, quality of life, disposable income, business environment or taxes, Canada has not only caught up to the United States, in many ways it has surpassed it. One major distinction, the foreign born population of Canada is 20%, while in the United States it stands at 13% (according to OECD).

Canada, by many measures, has the most successful immigration policy in the world.

Canada has become the destination of choice for educated, highly skilled immigrants who can immediately become productive members of the society. Canada uses a points system as the core for admitting new immigrant entrants. Applicants are awarded points for education, for foreign language skills, advanced degrees, types of degrees, and job experience. Moreover, Canada regularly updates its points system to accurately reflect what the countries needs are and are expected to be.

Much like the United States, the twentieth century was very fruitful for Canada, which along with the United States grew in economic strength and global prominence. As a result of the good fortunes of the last century, Canada has rightfully determined that as a result of its prominence and strength that it can "cherry pick" which immigrants it wants to become part of the national fabric. There is no prerequisite to have a job in hand, just the right skills, knowledge and experience to have the odds in your favor. Unlike most countries in the world, including the United States, Canada is focused on ensuring that it flourishes in the twenty-first century as well. Policy makers there understand that the decisions made today will greatly influence the future.

Why does Canada do this? Because it has to! Much like the United States, Canada has a declining birth rate, aging population and a generous social welfare system. Canada needs immigrants to boost its population, drive economic growth and ensure that the successes of the past century continue well into the future. In 2011, nearly two-thirds of the immigrant visas granted came as a result of economic need. In the United States, the opposite holds true – only one-third of Green Cards handed out where for economic reasons. The rest were almost awarded as part of our Family Reunification Policy.

Naturally, it is difficult to ensure that the skills of today are still relevant tomorrow. To address this, Canada offers continuing education classes to all its citizens, including immigrants. Moreover, Canada also provides "integration" classes to its immigrant populations, allowing immigrants to learn the intricacies of the Canadian culture. The purpose of the program is to improve the odds that an educated immigrant for the middle-east – let's say an engineer -- gets to work as an engineer in Canada as quickly as possible, as opposed to being a janitor or waiter. Canada's economy is thriving, because it not only welcomes immigrants, but also makes great efforts to see that these immigrants fully integrate into Canadian society, and are able to work in the highest paying jobs they are qualified for.

The United States needs to develop a flexible immigration policy that is based on economic and employment needs. Our failure to do so has cost our beloved country enormously. Failure to do so now could cause irreparable long-term damage to our economy and ability to compete in a global market place.

CHAPTER 2

The root of the economic problem

Demographics:

As a money manager and someone who runs an investment advisory firm, I spend countless hours speaking with clients and potential clients about investment strategies and how they relate to their goals, objectives and risk tolerance. When it comes to risk, I always point out to them that the biggest risk all of us face, regardless of how well off we are, is outliving our money. Sadly, for many people, this risk is very real. The reason is fairly simple: we are living longer, spending more, and in many cases are finding ourselves supporting a younger generation. Some experts are referring to my generation, people in their 40's and 50's as the "sandwich generation" – because we are supporting our children and our parents or grandparents. Economists refer to the ratio of the working age population (age 18 to 65) on the one side and the young (under age 18) and elderly (over age 59) as the "dependency ratio". By 2030, the year that children born this year (2012) will turn eighteen, the dependency ratio could reach 73, meaning that 73 out of 100 Americans will be dependent on the remaining 27 within the working age group. By way of comparison, in 1950 the dependency ratio was below 40, and reached 59 by 2005. Because our birthrate has essentially remained constant over the past 70 years, and we continue to live longer, the trend will continue and the dependency rate will continue to rise.

Working-Age Population by Race and Ethnicity,
Actual and Projected: 1960, 2005 and 2050

(% share of population ages 18 to 64)

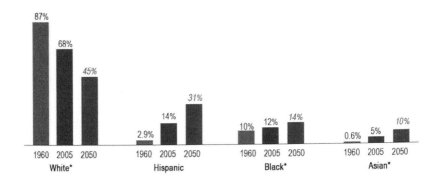

Note: All races modified and not Hispanic (*); American Indian/Alaska Native not shown.
See "Methodology." Projections for 2050 indicated by light brown bars.
Source: Pew Research Center, 2008

Whenever I talk with people about demographics and our demographic challenges, and what it means to us economically, I talk about the age pyramid. I find the fastest way to explain it is to make an upside down pyramid with my hands or draw it on a piece of paper. Whether they imagine it or see it, people can understand something precarious is at work. Pyramids, at least sustainable ones, are meant to be big part at the bottom, small part at the top. This one isn't.

The thick part represents seniors and the Medicare and social security they need to live their ever longer lives. The pointy part represents young people (even newborns) and the amount they pay into Medicare and Social Security. In the middle is a swath of the middle aged people paying upward for all those seniors and trying to fill up the coffers for themselves and their children. It is almost immediately evident to people that the pyramid is going to fall over unless something is done, namely, a whole lot more people coming in at the wedge end of the structure.

Spending too has inverted. Entitlement growth over the past 50 years has been astronomical – up 727%, after adjusting for population growth and inflation. In 1960, government outlays for social security, Medicare, Medicaid and other entitlements amounted to roughly one-third of the Federal Governments outlays; in 2010 entitlement spending had grown to represent roughly two-thirds of outlays. These increases are unsustainable.

In 1950 the United States had a population of 152 million. By 2010, the US population grew to just under 312 million people, and it is projected to reach 438 million by 2050. Although our overall population has grown, it has done so unevenly. Since World War II our birth rate has remained somewhat steady, averaging about 2 children per household. However, as a whole, our nation has grown older and continues to do so. According to several reports released in 2011 and 2012 by The Pew Research Center, Social Security Trustees and other groups, the elderly population of the United States "will more than double in size from 2005 through 2050." In part as a result of this rapid growth in our elderly population, the latest report by the Social Security Trust states that "legislative action is needed as soon as possible to prevent exhaustion of the (Disability Insurance) Trust Fund." The report further warns "if lawmakers do not take substantial action over the next few years, then changes necessary to maintain Social Security solvency will be concentrated on fewer years and fewer generations." One proposed solution by the trustees of Social Security is that "They (lawmakers) could increase the payroll tax rate to about 16.7% …or could reduce scheduled benefits by 25%." In other words, cut benefits by one -fourth and raise four fold the amount we pay into the system – good luck getting that passed in a politically polarized environment where half the law makers in the land believe that taxes should never go up.

The combination of steady birthrates, aging population and the slowdown in the growth of the labor force are the economic equivalent of a hurricane, tornado and earthquake hitting us all at once. The greatest challenge America will face over the next 25 to 30 years is addressing the significant demographic shift, and all of its economic implications, that is occurring.

We are all aware that by most projections, Social Security coffers and Medicaid and Medicare programs will run out of money sometime in the next 20 to 30 years – depending on how you do the math, and what assumptions you make. One thing is certain: no one believes the current system is good or sustainable. Nevertheless,, the discussions so far have been focused on which benefits need to be reduced or eliminated, and how high to raise taxes, a polarizing battle that is unlikely to make any real progress.

Researchers, including the Social Security Administration, calculate that the future of our population growth and with it much of our future economic growth will come from immigration. The steady birth rate is insufficient to counteract the effects of our aging population. Simply put, we are getting older and living longer. Now that the Baby Boomers have started to turn 60, and are entering retirement age, they are beginning to receive social security check. As a result of improved diets, exercise and medical improvements, our nation's elders are living much longer, placing a greater burden on our social security system. Economically speaking, our current system is operating under the following conditions: More people will need more money for longer; funded by fewer and fewer tax payers.

April 23, 2012: The Board of Trustees of the Federal Old-Age and Survivors Insurance and Federal Disability Insurance Trust Funds (Social Security / Medicare / Medicaid) – "Assets of The Disability Insurance Trust Fund decline steadily, fall below 100 percent of annual costs by the beginning of 2013, and continue to decline until the trust fund is exhausted in 2016." And "The Trustees project... that the dollar level of the combined trust funds (SS / MC / MA) declines beginning in 2021 until assets are exhausted in 2033." In other words, within a few months, our social security program will begin to deplete its assets and begin a rapid downward spiral.

Elderly Population by Race and Ethnicity, Actual and Projected:
1960, 2005 and 2050

(% share of population ages 65 years and older)

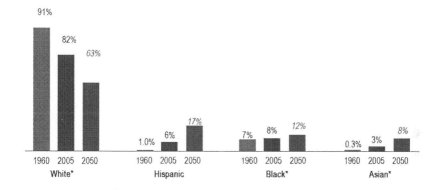

Note: All races modified and not Hispanic (*); American Indian/Alaska Native not shown.
See"Methodology." Projections for 2050 indicated by light brown bars.
Source: Pew Research Center, 2008

From a business perspective, it is obvious that this "business" is in real trouble and needs to take radical and aggressive steps if it hopes to survive.

Opponents of immigration reform, or really opponents of immigrants, will argue that by getting rid of illegal immigrants, the United States will be able to reduce social services costs to return the system to solvency. This, of course, is a fallacy. The truth is that based on our current mortality rate and birthrate, the population of the United States, excluding immigrants, will cease growing by 2025 or 2030. That may not sound so bad, but it is a real cause for alarm (remember what's happening in Japan right now).

Baby boomers, people born after WWII (1946) are beginning to turn 65, retirement age. According to the US Census Bureau, the number of Americans 55 or older will just about double in the next

19

19 years – from 60 million to 108 million. Or, to put it another way, the proportion of people facing retirement in our country will grow from 21% of the population to 31% in the next 2 decades. By 2040, almost 40% of Americans will be over age 50, with almost one-third of them over age 65.

The Pew Research Center projects that the number of elderly in the United States will "grow more rapidly that either the number of children or working-age adults. Immigration and births to immigrants in the United States will be responsible for all the growth of other age groups but will have little impact on the number of elderly, which is affected mainly by the aging of the post-World War II baby-boom generation." At the same time, the American Medical Association, in conjunction with the AARP, estimates that about half of the people age 65 will live into their nineties. And the number of Americans over age 85 will double by 2030.

Of course, the future and our economic trajectory can be altered by our economic and social policies, including, and most urgently, our immigration policy. The Trustees of the Social Security Trust have incorporated immigration assumptions into their long-term projections. According to their projections, reducing "new" immigration by 25%, the costs per American worker for Social Security would rise nearly 40%. Conversely, by increasing immigration by 25%, the cost of Social Security per American worker would drop by 35%. Unfortunately, even with a 25% increase in immigration, there will still be a shortfall in the Social Security coffers. This is partially due to the Trustees assumptions that are based on the continued trend of low-skill, low-wage immigration, as opposed to being more pragmatic and deliberate by encouraging high-skilled, high-wage (read high tax revenue) immigrants to migrate to the United States.

Some have proposed, or resigned themselves to the idea that they will have to work longer in life, that retirement at age 60 or 65 is simply no longer a viable option. "70 is the new 50" some profess, but that too brings a significant set of problems. Unless we have a vibrant economy, there may not be enough jobs for seniors wanting and needing to work later into life, and college graduates seeking employment. What type of choices will we as a society face then?

A recent study by the RAND Institute and the University of Michigan reveal that as a result of the aging population, and the "natural" increase in disabilities, illness', and frailty, the cost associated with our aging citizens could increase by as much as $4 trillion over the next 30 years.

There is only one way to change and ultimately reverse that trend – we need more young people who are in the work force. Or to put it another way, we need more tax revenues, lots more tax revenues. It is mathematically impossible to reconcile our current deficits and projected deficits and debt servicing costs with higher taxes from our current citizens. There are simple not enough Americans paying enough taxes to fix the burden. Arguments that cost cuts and inefficiencies in the system need to be address are absolutely correct. Proposals to curb benefits for the wealthy, even though they paid into the system, may also need to be part of the solution – but even these two approaches combined will not address the problem in a sufficient manner. There is only one way – more tax payers, significantly more.

A Closer Look at The Age Pyramid

Throughout the history of the world, various populations have in essence resembled a pyramid. Lots of young people (under age 12), a few less 13 to 18 years olds, a few less 19 to 35 year olds, fewer 35 to 55 year olds and a small fraction – historically less than 10% of the population has been above age 55 (keeping in mind that in 1900, the life expectancy for the average European was 46 years; it is now over 76 years). Over time, for a variety of factors including decreasing birthrates, improvements in medicine and better diets our life expectancy has increased. As I was once asked by a philosophy professor: "What is the meaning of life"? I smugly answered "avoidance of death". I was a smart-ass, but there is much truth in this answer. We work out at the gym, eat healthier, take various medications, all in an effort to delay the inevitable, and all leading to greater longevity.

Today, this age pyramid has been reversed, or at the very least somewhat flattened and is in the process of being put upside-down. This absolutely needs to be addressed, and there are few viable solutions. (Russia is facing an even greater problem of the "inverted pyramid." In the early 1990's they attempted to pay their citizens to take time off during lunch and make babies. This did not have any measurable impact on Russia's birth rate). The solution, whatever it ends up being, needs to result in more 18 to 40 year olds who will work for many years and pay taxes for many years. Although it might be tempting to point to other nations and express how much worse they have it, this approach does nothing to help us.

The first baby boomer was born about one second after midnight on January 1st, 1946. Her name is Kathleen Casey-Kirschling. She turned 65 on January 1, 2011 and with her came a wave of retirees who moved from an asset accumulation to an asset distribution phase of their economic lives. More broadly speaking, this also ushered in a significant change in our nations demographics - the great switchover and inversion of the age pyramid in the United States. The aging of our population has significant economic implications. Retirees economic role in society changes, although they still consume goods and services, they stop producing them. Ergo, half of their previous economic contribution to society is eliminated, and they stop contributing to GDP growth.

Moreover, in a traditional form of retirement, people deplete their assets. They spend down their savings, because that is what they live off and rightfully so. They have done their job. None-theless, the economic implications from this are significant. Some will say that they plan on working into their 70's, or that they will "do" some sort of consulting work. The truth of it is that no matter how you slice it, when you retire – fully or partially, your economic contribution to a society slows and diminishes.

According to the Social Security Administration, the average life-expectancy today is 76 and by 2030 it will be over age 85. The concept of social security was first introduced to the world by Germany, in the late 1800's. At the time, the life expectancy in Germany was about 46 years. The government promised its citizens that in return for a slight increase in taxes now, they would be awarded and guaranteed an income in their retirement years. They knew that on turning 60 that as long as there were many people paying into the system and only a few drawing from it, that all would be well. Today, of course, the opposite holds true: We have fewer and fewer people paying into the system, and more drawing from it, and they are drawing from it for much longer than originally envisioned.

Social Security and Census bureau officials estimate that by 2050, the United States could have between 200 and 240 million additional people who will require some form of elderly care. The cumulative outlays for Medicare, Medicaid and Social Security are going to be absolutely staggering, and it is not something that can be fixed with increasing tax on the wealthy or simply cutting the expenditures. Therein lies an enormous problem.

There is not enough disposable income available, nor are there enough tax revenues available based on our demographics to solve this issue. You cannot cut the benefits on enough people to greatly affect this problem. I suppose you could argue that if you have a net worth over a certain sum, or you have an income over a certain sum, you are not eligible for Social Security, for Medicare and Medicaid. The trouble is you are still asking these people to pay into the system, and quite a few people are going to cry "foul!" Under this type of system, the wealthy will likely leave the United States and take their precious tax dollars with them, accelerating the problem. But even if fairness was not an issue, the problem would not go away.

As a result of our aging population, increasing "dependency rate" and the resulting increased need and demand for government sponsored and tax payer funded social program, our national account deficits will continue to increase – unless we come up with a way to significantly increase our taxpayer base and lower the "dependency rate." From an investment perspective, the smaller working age population will have to save more to meet their financial goals. In the meantime, seniors are likely to have to begin selling their assets (stocks, bonds, etc.) to meet their lifestyle goals. This too could have a detrimental impact on expected returns from investments.

U.S. Population, Actual and Projected: 2005 and 2050		
	2005	**2050**
Population (in millions)	296	438
Share of total		
Foreign born	12%	19%
Racial / Ethnic Groups		
White	67%	47%
Hispanic	14%	29%
Black	13%	13%
Asian	5%	9%
Age Groups		
Children (17 and younger)	25%	23%
Working (18 - 64)	63%	58%
Elderly (65 and older)	12%	19%
Note: All races modified and not Hispanic (*); American Indian / Alaska Native not shown. See"Methodology." Source: Pew Research Center, 2008		

Keep in mind that inflation is going to play a role in all of this as well. There are some pretty terrifying forces at work. Let us imagine for a moment that you need $60,000 gross a year to live, leaving aside taxes for the moment. Let's pretend for a moment that when you are a senior, you somehow do not owe any taxes anymore, so you can live on $60,000 a year in 2012/2013 dollars. At a very, very low inflation rate of two percent—and I think most will agree that it is likely to be higher than that—20 years from now that will require $90,000 to have the same buying power. As costs naturally rise with inflation and greater demand for goods and services from countries outside the United States, we may be faced with a reality of decreasing asset and investment values.

Never before have we been faced with the problems that we are facing today. Throughout history, people have migrated to opportunity – in the 1800's and 1900's people migrated to the United States because of opportunity. Today, we are nearing the point when people will leave e United States to find opportunity elsewhere. We can avoid this fate, but we must act deliberately and consciously to avert an inversion of the age pyramid.

What does that mean in for the immigration discussion? Simply put, you can only grow your way out of this issue. We can only grow our way out of the debt, out of the deficit, and out of the inversion of the age pyramid. The United States, just like Japan and Europe, needs economic growth and population growth. Given our steady birthrates but rising dependency rate as the result of the aging of our population, we need to rely on immigration to address this issue. We are not having enough babies as a country to achieve it on our own.

A recent study by the Center for American Progress shows that a comprehensive immigration reform that focuses on economic and employment needs first, is estimated to generate "an increased in U.S. GDP of at least 0.84 percent." Summed over 10 years this amounts to a cumulative $1.5 trillion in additional GDP. It also boosts wages for both native-born and newly legalized immigrant workers.' Conversely, the study also shows that our current policy, which is focused on deportation, is likely to cost the U.S. economy over $2.6 trillion or 1.46 percent in cumulative GDP over 10 years.

Here's the rub. We will continue to age, and by adding to our immigrant population, they will age too. Who will pay for them? We will, of course. There is no choice. This is precisely why we need to develop long-term economic strategies that incorporate immigration, education and social policy reforms to address our problems.

It is easy to dismiss these challenges by making callous thoughtless statements such as "oh well, they'll just have to do with less," or "then there's just no Social Security or Medicare anymore." These are unrealistic sentiments, impractical if not outright impossible. Just ask yourself this: What if it was you, or your mother and father, son or daughter who is among the "sorry, nothing for you" group. It's easy to cut someone else's benefits, but cutting your own – not quite as easy, and certainly not as pleasant.

To convince the skeptics, let's do the math: If we were to remove Social Security, just let it run out of money as it will by 2033, we will be reducing disposable income and thereby GDP in the United States by some $200 billion, roughly 1 ½% to 2% of current GDP.

As our population ages the need for medical treatment will increase. According to the April 2012 report by the Social Security Trustees, the Disability Trust will begin depleting its assets in 2013, and will run out of money (unless corrective action is taken) by 2016. Social Security and other programs face a similar, fast-approaching, fate.

According to official projections, to ensure that modernized versions of these programs exist in the future, the United States will need to raise, at minimum, an additional 53 billion dollars in annual revenues to pay for them. This cannot be done by raising taxes and unless we fully eliminate welfare, food stamps, social security, Medicare and Medicaid, we will still be in the red. For those of you who are nodding and say "well, then we eliminate them," think about what you are suggesting and recognize that we will be the only western nation on the planet without these social safety nets, and will be at par with Ghana, Cote D'Ivoire and some other small African nations who rely on UNICEF and the United Nations for food distribution to their population – not a place or environment I aspire to be in. The bottom line, we need to generate and extra 53 billion dollars in revenue, which will likely take an extra 40 million taxpayers.

CHAPTER 3

The politics and economics of immigration:To some, immigration is already a business

America has a choice. We can make immigration our business, or we can let it keep taking our business and tax dollars away, while at the same time funding a business that few of us want to fund. Here's what I mean.

The U.S. – Mexican border stretches for hundreds of miles. The days are long, the sun is hot and the wind spits dust in your face. Everyday border agents do their best to monitor their assigned area and capture people trying to cross illegally. In the Tucson sector, according to a recent set of interviews of border patrol agents on the television news show 20/20, agents are capturing between 200 and 400 individuals a day. Along this stretch, agents play a high stakes game of hide and seek with migrants trying to enter the United States illegally. Once caught, they are typically arrested and then become an entry on a prison company's balance sheet. From San Diego, through Arizona, all the way to Dallas, along the I-10 corridor, detention centers are popping up everywhere and it is big business.

Steve Afeman of Emerald Correctional Management says demand is so high, that just four years after opening a new detention center in San Luis, Arizona, they are laying the foundation for another wing. "We will grow a minimum of 15 to 20 percent a year over the next 5 years, straight," says Afeman.

Immigration detention is the new area of growth for those in the prison business. The number of detained immigrants on any given day has swelled to more than 30,000, about half of them in private facilities. Many are deported after only a few days, but others can remain in custody for months or years. There are a couple of reasons for the vast differences in the length of detention of an illegal immigrant. Depending on space availability, immigrants might get shipped to a detention center several hundred, sometimes thousands of miles away from where they were captured. This of course, greatly affects the processing and eventual deportation time. Also, depending on where they were caught, and for what reason, our current immigration policy requires immigrants who work here to purchase their own plane ticket home. Illegal immigrants who do not have the money to pay for the airfare, typically about $1,600, remain in the detention center until they can come up with the money. Although some might be tempted to say "good – at least they can pay for their own way home," the cost to tax payers for keeping illegal immigrants in these centers is about $125 per day. In other words, the cost of the airfare is less than 2 weeks in a private prison. Many are kept in these detention centers for over a year.

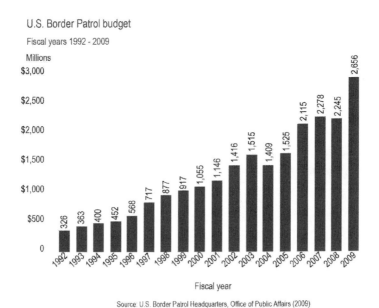

U.S. Border Patrol budget

Fiscal years 1992 - 2009

Millions

Fiscal year

Source: U.S. Border Patrol Headquarters, Office of Public Affairs (2009)

They include Brenda Ambrosio who says she came to the U.S. in 2001 to escape her abusive husband in Guatemala. She knows she broke the law but says she had no other place to turn. In an interview, she admits that she broke the law, but adds "I went to find out about asylum in Mexico, but I could not get anything... escaping to America was my only chance for survival." Ambrosio is one of the 12 million undocumented immigrants in the U.S. Her story might be unusual, but the outcome certainly isn't. While living in Maryland, she worked two jobs, remarried and had a daughter born in America. But then, a minor traffic violation brought Brenda out of the shadows. While driving to work, Ambrosio inadvertently did not signal a right turn. The police officer behind her put the lights on and pulled her over. Eventually, Ambrosio was sent 2300 miles away from her family to Arizona inside the Eloy Detention Center.

Eloy is owned and operated by the Corrections Corporation of America, CCA. Immigrants have an important place in CCA's corporate history and helped the company get its first contract in 1984. Detention facilities like Eloy bring in about 12-percent of CCA's revenue or 200 million dollars (of tax payer money) a year. Private prison companies are responding to the demand created by the nation's immigration laws. But critics allege the companies are doing something more, something legal but troubling: trying to promote immigration laws that pad their bottom lines.

Andrea Black leads the Detention Watch Network, a coalition of immigrant advocacy groups. She is of the view that although private prison companies may be following federal immigration law, it is a law that they have heavily influenced. She cites records showing CCA has spent nearly 19 million dollars lobbying federal officials, much of it directed at agencies that oversee immigration policy. The company staunchly denies it lobbies policy makers on immigration enforcement or sentencing laws – my response is "of course not." From an economic perspective, the immigrant detention programs in the United States have reached crisis levels. Over the past 15 years, detention centers have grown nearly fourfold in size, growing from 6,300 beds in 1996 to over 33,500 beds at the end of 2010. Because many of those who are locked up are families with young children, victims of human trafficking, malnourished migrants and elderly people, the cost of care for them is significant.

On any given day, the Department of Homeland Security spends an average of $5.5 million taxpayer dollars on detaining immigrants. As our country debates spending cuts, including reducing or even eliminating programs such as extended unemployment benefits and the food stamp program, the Obama administration has requested over $2 billion in funding for immigrant detention in 2012.

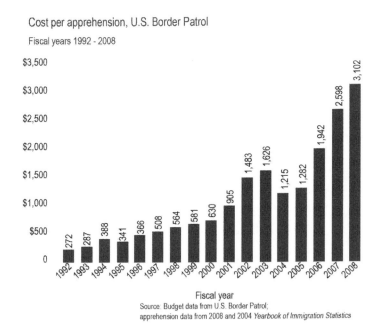

Cost per apprehension, U.S. Border Patrol

Fiscal years 1992 - 2008

Fiscal year
Source: Budget data from U.S. Border Patrol;
apprehension data from 2008 and 2004 *Yearbook of Immigration Statistics*

Moreover, absent a strong lobbying force by the private prison companies, detention centers for illegal immigrants are in essence unnecessary and outdated. Those caught and verified as being illegal immigrants could be deported within hours or days, at a cost of a few dollars per day, instead of the high cost of detention centers. Over the past few years, the stock price of CCA and its peers has certainly reflected to bright outlook of their business. CCA shares (ticker CXW) have gained nearly 50% in 2012, far outpacing the S&P 500, which returned about 16%, including dividends (investor darling Apple, had a 40 percent-ish return in 2012). Our current system, line of thinking and recent laws, such as the one in Alabama, or Arizona State Senate Bill 1070, do ensure one thing – they help drive growth and almost insure that CCA and companies like it will have a steady stream of new customers. Senate Bill 1070, for example, is measure that grants law enforcement expanded powers to check people's immigration status. The bill's chief sponsor is Senate President Russell Pearce. He is a supporter of private prison companies. And, guess what? They are a supporter of him.

These guys have found a way to exploit the fundamentally flawed immigration policy for their profit. But they only prosper at the expense of the economy and the future. And, of course, the more the whole system becomes entrenched, the harder it is going to be to shift.

A sensible and smart immigration policy will foster growth, strengthen our economy and build a stronger society. Detention centers profits will suffer, but I, for one, will take it as a sign that America has come to its senses.

The economics of Immigration:

While private prison companies like CCA are benefiting from our current immigration policies, at the cost of tax payers, America is limited in its economic gains from the current policies. The broad question is this: are there steps we can take to improve the economic gains the United States is making from immigration. As a starting point, we must recognize that immigration is a global and constant phenomenon. People migrate to opportunity; they do not just migrate across the globe at random. There are certain industries that attract more immigrants and much depends on the level of education. Restaurants, hospitals, hotels, construction, farms, labor intensive manufacturing all attract manual labor. In the United States, that population is predominately made up of South-American, Latin-American and Mexican migrant workers. The reason is, in part, because we as Americans do not want those jobs as can be easily documented by the experience of Alabama. Farming highlights the problem because farming is a very time-sensitive industry that requires labor at a specific point in time and for a specific period of time. That is why, by the way, we have instituted policies, and rightfully so, that specifically allow migrant workers to come in and then exit the United States to help with the farming of tomatoes, carrots, berries and whatever else.

Our current focus on detention and deportation is not only costly, it is also very damaging to our economy. Americans who complain that illegal immigration drives wages lower have a partial point – it does, to an extent. But it does so because of our focus on detention and deportation. The reality is that the side effect of our current "enhanced" enforcement policy is that it forces more illegal immigrants underground, "lowering their wages and ironically, creating a greater demand for unauthorized workers." A 2008 report by the Atlanta Federal Reserve analyzed this phenomenon and concluded that when a firm cuts costs by hiring unauthorized workers for lower wages, its competitors become more likely to hire illegal immigrants as well, a vicious, undesirable cycle for certain.

When we carefully consider the 12 million or so undocumented and illegal immigrants in the United States, we have to recognize that they present a tremendous opportunity. According to the American Community Survey of the Census Bureau, there are about 38.5 million foreign born Americans in 2009. The figures were 9.6 million or 4.7% in 1970, so it has risen sharply and that is probably one of the main reasons why the debate about immigration has become so politicized and feverish. That title cannot change so long as we view immigration as a problem rather than a solution.

The truth is that the number of jobs in our economy is not finite but is rather highly elastic, meaning that the more consumption there is, the more we grow our economy, and subsequently, the greater number of jobs we will create. It is the classic "chicken before the egg" debate. However, it is misguided to pretend or stipulate that immigrants are taking American jobs. Not so. There is zero evidence of this - because the jobs that they are taking at the current pay levels would simply go unfilled. American's are not willing to take them. Of course, the argument can be made that if the pay for these jobs would rise sufficiently, Americans would take them. But this would make many of our industries such as agriculture, tourism, hospitality and the food and beverage industry very uncompetitive. Which would you pick? The $10 California grapes or $4 Chilean grapes? Would you vacation in Florida if hotel rooms cost $500 per night, as a result of high labor costs, or would you go to Mexico where the same room type from the same hotel chain costs you $200 per night? Remember, you're not earning more – how far will your dollar stretch?

The development of immigration policy affects not only national security and other priorities, but most importantly our economy. Overly restrictive policy has the potential to devastate certain industries which would be faced with near crisis conditions in terms of affordable labor. In fact, millions of jobs are at stake and the spillover effect ripples through every sector of our economy and every region in the country.

The economic impact of eliminating all undocumented workers from our workforce for the U.S. as a whole would be as follows: about one and three quarter trillion dollars of annual loss spending, about six hundred and fifty billion dollars in annual lost output, and about eight million lost jobs – this represents a greater loss than the much dreaded "fiscal-cliff" the United States faced at the end of 2012. It represents the equivalent of the economic conditions America experienced during the Great Depression in the 1930's. Should our economy recover from the impact of lost economic activity and growth resulting from deporting all illegal immigrants, we would still face our most serious and fundamental problem – our aging population which relies on tax payer funded social services. Kicking out illegal immigrants will accelerate and deepen the problem, not solve it. We need to remember that many of the undocumented workers pay Social Security taxes, adding to our budget. They do this knowing that under the current system they will never be able to collect any of the monies they are paying into the Social Security coffers. Most estimates are that approximately 7.5 million undocumented immigrants pay FICA taxes. Eliminating these revenues would remove as much as $7 billion in tax revenues per year.

According to recent demographic and migration trend research by the Pew Hispanic Center, our weak housing market and overall sluggish economy has caused significant job losses in construction and the hospitality business, both of which attract many immigrants. And as we have indicated, signs are that immigration is drying up and is even in reverse.

Let's take California, our nations' largest state and biggest contributor to our overall economy. Recently, California Farm Bureau President Paul Wenger testifies at a House subcommittee hearing in Washington, D.C., that farmers and their employees need practical, effective immigration solutions. California's economy heavily depends on its agriculture business, and so does our entire nation. Absent an immigration program which facilitates the legal employment of foreign worker on U.S. farms and ranches, the States' agricultural business would suffer great harm – it would be "a disaster for American agriculture." Proposals like the new E-Verify program place significant regulatory and bureaucratic burdens on our farmers – something you would think Republicans who want less government oversight and involvement in private industry would be staunchly against.

In testimony before a hearing of the House Judiciary Subcommittee on Immigration Policy and Enforcement in Washington, D.C., California Farm Bureau President Paul Wenger said farmers rely on an immigrant workforce and many of their employees might not qualify to work under the system known as E-Verify.

"Last year, this committee approved a bill that would make E-Verify mandatory for all employers regardless of size or industry; however, it offered no solution to address the unique challenges that a national E-Verify mandate will create for agriculture,"Wenger said. "E-Verify, without a workable, economical way to ensure a legal agricultural workforce, will send American agricultural production, and the additional off-farm jobs that are created by it, to other countries."

E-Verify legislation sponsored by House Judiciary Committee Chairman Lamar Smith, R-Texas, would require employers to verify the eligibility of prospective employees before hiring. The electronic system checks against Social Security numbers and Department of Homeland Security records.

Another witness at the hearing, Georgia Agriculture Commissioner Gary Black, joined Wenger in telling the House panel that without a solution in place, passage of a proposed employment-verification rule would be disruptive to agriculture.

"Without twenty-first century guest-worker program that includes many of the initiatives that are contained in pending legislation, I see no way for farmers to meet the future consumer demand with domestically produced peppers (such as in our state) and other agricultural products," said Black, whose state began requiring private employers to use E-Verify last year.

"Nationally, it is estimated that the agricultural workforce consists of 1.83 million hired workers and some have estimated that as much as 50% to 70% of the hired workers are not authorized to work in the United States," Wenger said. "Agriculture needs a timely solution that fills the gap between the currently legally authorized workforce and the agricultural needs of the nation."

Rep. Zoe Lofgren, D-San Jose, asked Wenger if it is possible to replace the current agricultural workforce. Wenger replied that the workforce is made up of thousands of skilled employees.

"A lot of the folks doing this work are driving pieces of equipment that are worth more than your most expensive Mercedes," Wenger said. "They are highly skilled people and understand what they are doing, so it is paramount that we give them some kind of adjustment of status to allow them to be in this country and work."

The bottom line, regardless of which industry we talk about, is that we need a comprehensive immigration policy that matches our labor needs and the labor pool. We must take an approach that places current and future economic needs ahead of ideology. Just as importantly, we have to have a long-term perspective and plan and that must include a revision of our education system, from middle school through college. Ensuring that we have an educated, skilled population is one of the keys to our economic prosperity.

We have made some progress on the issue, albeit with heavy political scars. In July 2012, President Obama issued an executive order that lifted the threat of deportation for illegal immigrants who were brought to or entered the United States before the age of sixteen and are still under the age of thirty one, and have been in the U.S. for at least five years. Most of the 800,000 or so immigrants that fall into this category are high school students and members of our military. The basis of the new policy, with which I agree completely, is that those affected are here as a result of someone else's actions and are not responsible for their illegal status. President Obama emphasized that this is not an amnesty program, but rather a mechanism to allow young people to remain in a country that has in many cases been their home for most of their lives. While announcing the executive order, President Obama stated that "they do not deserve to be treated like criminals or uprooted from the only country they've known. They are Americans in their heart, in their minds, in every single way but one: on paper," he said. The President conceded that this was only a stop-gap measure and that more needs to be done – including asking Congress to take another look at the Dream Act (originally a bipartisan bill).

There is no doubt that politics played and will continue to play a significant role in this debate. Prior to the 2012 elections, several thousand are delaying signing up until after the election because they fear that the Republicans might in some way repeal or scale back the program thus leaving them exposed to deportation because of the information they would have provided. I suspect that as the next election cycle approaches, both sides will likely continue to harden their rhetoric and use this as a hockey puck to gain voters favor. Unfortunately, the biggest point, and opportunity is being missed – "it's the economy" as Bill Clinton famously said in 2000.

Certain industries are of course, much more susceptible and dependent on undocumented workers than others. The restaurant, hospitality and housing industries pretty much tell the story.

Advocates of the enforcement and "ship them out policy" often rely on statements and arguments that immigrants tend to heavily rely on social services, more than our native born population. Not true. The eligibility restrictions for undocumented immigrants prevent them from enrolling in most programs.

So although it is true that almost 33% of immigrant household use and a major welfare program, which is significantly higher than 19% of native born Americans, most of those are not from the undocumented population. It goes back to a question of the level of education and poverty involved because that is what is really driving the need and the use of the social welfare programs.

Of course, the level of immigrants within the immigrant population—undocumented immigrants—varies widely by state. States like California, New York, New Jersey, Florida, have historically had the highest number of immigrants overall. However, Arizona, by way of comparison, has the highest percentage of undocumented workers as a share of the workforce. It stands at 12% which is roughly double the national average. That is why, or at least it is a partial explanation for the even more emotional reaction of people in that state when discussions about illegal immigration and undocumented workers are raised.

It is important when having this debate to recognize that most or all undocumented workers and illegal immigrants pay sales taxes. They pay property taxes. And in many cases, through their work, they pay social security taxes and FICA taxes without being able to take advantage of the corresponding benefit. In other words, an undocumented worker working under a false social security number pays into the system, but will never be able to collect social security. As such, the overall level of taxes they pay adds to the U.S. economy, even on a regional and local level. These dollars offset the costs of the social services including schooling for their children and other benefits.

If all undocumented workers were removed from the workforce, a number of industries would face substantial shortages of workers. Americans would somehow have to be induced into the labor pool through incentives to take jobs far below their current education and skill level. For this phenomenon to occur to a meaningful extent, substantial wage escalation would likely be necessary, thus eroding competitiveness in the global markets.

Immigrants, and in particular, undocumented workers fill a number of important jobs in the U.S. especially in the service sector, construction and farming. As the domestic workforce becomes older as baby boomers age and as it becomes more stable in number and better educated, the U.S. production sector increasingly needs foreign, low-skilled workers. Currently the economy is relying on more low-skilled immigrant workers than the allowable work visas in current policy. We need to change the policy. Here's why.

In 1960, about 50% of men in this country joined the low-skilled labor force without completing high school. The number today is less than 10%. While a more educated workforce is certainly a positive development that has contributed to growth, productivity and improved standards of living, there are still low-skilled jobs that need to be filled. In fact, with the retirement of many boomers beginning in 2008, long-term projections from the U.S. Bureau of Labor Statistics indicate that about 60% of future requirements will be replacements rather than new positions. Moreover, most of these jobs will be in service industries and about 70% will be at relatively low skill levels. The total demand will far exceed the rate of growth in the workforce that will occur from natural expansion and the entry afforded by current immigration policy, leaving a potential gap of tens of millions of laborers. Even if expected advances in technology reduce the shortages and some marginal workers are induced into the workforce from other sources, the need for an immigrant pool to perform these functions is likely to increase over time as the economy grows. In short, immigrants, including those who are undocumented, are important to filling needs in the less skilled labor force, an area that the Bureau of Labor Statistics and government-sponsored think tanks project to grow substantially in the coming decade. The sure outcome is that although we are making vast strides in robotics and automation, the need for cheap unskilled labor will grow, not shrink. For several industries and occupations, undocumented immigrants serve as an important source of labor.

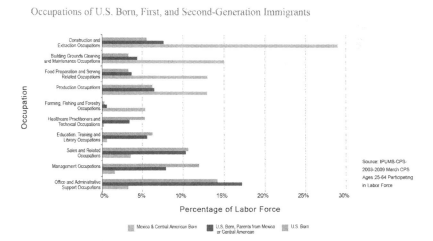

Occupations of U.S. Born, First, and Second-Generation Immigrants

But mark well the unintended consequences for ignoring these realities.. In August, 2011, a business executive from Mercedes-Benz, which employs thousands in its factories in Alabama, got caught in their unwelcome web. Detlev Hager was caught with only his German ID on him. As a result, the police detained him and he spent a couple of nights in one of Alabama's less than comfortable jails. Only when a colleague managed to retrieve his passport from the suitcase in his hotel room was he released. If I have anything to do with the management of Mercedes-Benz, I might be inclined to look for a more clement environment to spend my money. That could spell real trouble for the 54,000 Alabamans who are employed by foreign companies.

Most Americans would agree that one of the keys to a strong, vibrant America is having a strong manufacturing base. And no industry employs more people in manufacturing than the auto industry. The auto industry as a whole is comprised of roughly 141,000 business. More significantly, when accounting for the manufactures, suppliers and related businesses, the auto industry employs over 480,000 workers. In 1978, Volkswagen opened the first non-US auto assembly plant in the United States. Since then, the American auto industry has changed significantly. As of the end of 2009, there were 470 foreign-owned auto supply plants and 18 foreign-owned assembly plants – there are only 24 American owned assembly plants. If we "ban" immigrants, will we also ask foreign auto manufactures to keep their plants and the jobs at home – most certainly not! The reason of course is simple, "they" are good immigrants, because "they" bring skills, wealth and ultimately jobs to the table.

Times have changed, and in many cases so have our businesses and industries. Unfortunately, our immigration policies have not kept up with the globalization of the world. We are not alone, but that cannot be our measuring stick or excuse. Virtually all economist and policy makers agree that protectionism is bad policy in today's global market place. In order for the United States to remain competitive and to take advantage of the growing wealth of "emerging markets" we must be able to export, an outcome that will become increasingly difficult if we put up "One Way" signs in trade deals. "Closing our border is a twentieth-century thought, and it will only weaken the economy over the long term" said Andrew N. Liveris, president of

Dow Chemical and co-chairman of the Advanced Manufacturing Partnership, a group of executives and academics convened by the White House who are charged with developing proposals to increase manufacturing and manufacturing jobs in the United States.

An international perspective on immigration:

All nations in the world experience some form of immigration. In the case of the United States, as is typical for prosperous countries, immigrants want to come here. Other nations are the source of immigrants. Take for instance, the Philippines. The Philippines "exports" the largest number of people, in both relative and absolute terms, of any country in the world. Each year, over 1 million Filipinos leave their homeland for better economic opportunity somewhere else. The Philippines have a culture of migration and they are the third largest provider of migrant and immigrant workers to the United States. Some have argued that the Philippine government is simply growing and exporting its people like cash crop. That this deliberate exporting of humans is done for the sole purpose of planting seeds in other parts of the world in an effort to repatriate as many foreign earned monies from richer and more vibrant economies, such as the United States and Europe. That may well be true, but it doesn't change the fact that they have a deliberate immigration – or in this case migration policy, that is designed to benefit the Philippine economy. Their strength and talent in migration is helping their economy, while our ineptitude and short-sighted approach is hurting ours. The reason I am using the Philippines as an example is that they have enormous numbers people that who leave there. But the people in the Philippines are not tortured, nor mistreated, nor do they live under a dictatorship. On the contrary, it is quite pleasant there. They are moving to the U.S. and to Europe because it is an economic lifeline for them and it is a cultural norm. Of course, the wage differential is ultimately what drives it. The jobs pay more here in the U.S. and in Europe than they do back in the Philippines so they are able to send money back.

Repatriation of funds, monies being sent "home" occurs most prevalently when families are split. If the bread winner lives in one country, but the spouse and children remain home, monies will be sent to them – it's natural. Officially, in 2010 roughly $30 billion was taken out of the US economy and repatriated to immigrants' homelands. (This sum has been reasonably consistent over the past decade.) Unofficially, the amount could be twice as much, since the official government figures do not include most of the funds sent through Western Union and similar service providers. A more deliberate and inclusive immigration policy could help the United States keep some, if not most, of these dollars here to the benefit of us all.. The key is to figure out a sensible way to allow for the assimilation of our immigrant population, something that some countries are doing better than others.

We like to think that immigration is a unique American phenomenon. However, if you speak to people in Europe about immigration, they wonder why we have a problem with immigration in the U.S. Germans, for example, have a particularly large number of Turkish and northern Middle East, southeastern Europe and eastern European immigrants and they would characterize them as lazy, slow to fit into the culture and reluctant to assimilate. Sound familiar?

It's the same the world over – in most countries immigrants are considered people who do not fit in, do not assimilate and do not easily become part of the social fabric, at least not yet. This is almost always true, unless the country makes a great effort to assimilate immigrants – without racial or religious bias. I've previously mentioned Canada as a country that appears to have one of the most successful immigration policies in the world. As part of their policy initiatives, Canada has also taken numerous steps to ensure that first and second generation immigrants fully assimilate into society. Take Calgary as an example. Calgary is a modern metropolitan city, with major industries, a sophisticated public transportation system, and served as the host of the 1988 Winter Olympics. Most impressively,

Calgary also boasts one of the highest standards of living in the world. Calgary is home to more Latin American born engineers than any other city in North America, and has a Muslim mayor. Now that's what I call integration.

Canada is not the only country in the world that is keen on managing its immigration policies and their migration policies. Some countries in the world are not only encouraging immigration, they are actually paying people to stay in the country. Dubai's new skyline and the world's tallest building was built by immigrants. They are now starting to leave from Africa to go to Europe as opposed to Dubai because the economics have changed. Dubai is very keen on keeping a lot of that workforce and so they are paying people to stay. It is not an enormous amount of money for them, but fewer are leaving than otherwise would. In the Middle East, payments are being made to Palestinians to stay in the area for political considerations.

As for America, it should be clear to you by now that we're not exactly doing the best job with our immigration policy. It wasn't always so and it could be amazingly better. So it may be helpful to understand just how we got to the situation we're in.

CHAPTER 4

The history of immigration in the United States

The historical key to the wealth and power of the United States -- and for that matter, Canada, South Africa, Australia and Argentina -- has been immigration. And while those whose descendants came over on the Mayflower may occasionally forget it, even they were immigrants. In fact, before during and after these countries became independent powers, it was the flow of immigrants, predominantly from Europe at first, that so shaped their development.

All of these countries had land, natural resources and money. What they lacked was labor to do the farming, the lumbering, the mining, the and ultimately the manufacturing that would capitalize on the rich promise of the country. Of course, sadly, for such a long time that labor existed in the form of slavery, with untold consequences we still have yet to sort out. When cities began to be built not long after the end of the Civil War, it was the Germans and the Irish who provided the hands, the hours and the sweat. But they were not complaining because they were driven by the same motive as immigrants in our own day: the hope of a better life.

At first it was a trickle of people, but between 1820 and 1880, a flood of some 15 million immigrants (helped by the Napoleonic wars and in the 1840s by the potato famine in Ireland). The suspicion about Roman Catholics abounded but the need for labor trumped the Pope. Americans seemed not to begrudge the immigrants, though, as always, "no Irish" or "no Germans" signs appeared in places where people, having insured their own place, wanted to pull the ladder up.

In 1882, a sort of immigration policy occurred with the passage of the Chinese Exclusion Act. Well, at least they didn't wrap their prejudices in euphemisms back then. By the turn of the century the tide could not be turned as ship after ship from Europe, mainly, made its voyage to American soil and 25 million Europeans disembarked: Greeks, Italians, Poles and Jews, each clutching their dream and together forming the neighborhoods of ethnicity that we still can see today. It was the formative and defining period for America, not without abrasions, but urging a wider embracing of people who wanted to melt into the American Dream. This influx continued until about 1920.

Then in 1924 The National Origins Act of 1921 was finalized and restrictions (read: quotas) were written into the national policy. The bent of the policy was clearly for whites and western Europeans, at the same time limiting immigrants from Asia and southern Europe. Even so, immigrants from the Western Hemisphere had no quotas imposed so millions from Mexico, the Caribbean, including Jamaica, Barbados Haiti and other parts of Central and South America made their way to the United States.

All this changed with the passage of the Hart-Celler Act of 1965. A byproduct of the Civil Rights Movement, and part of President Lyndon Johnson's Great Society, the Hart-Celler Act intended to do away with the racially-based quota system that existed, and transform our immigration policy to be driven by skills and family reunification. This in essence is an early example of a progressive immigration policy that is designed to help our economy.

As a result of the passage of the act, there continued to be an influx of people from European countries but around 1970 those from Korea, China, India the Philippines and Pakistan, also found their way here. By the turn of the century, immigration had returned to its volume of 1900 and some people (those who are already securely here, of course) are shouting that the boat can't hold any more people. Much of the hostility towards immigrants is directed at Hispanics, in part because many people believe they are unwilling or unable to assimilate into American culture. But this has always been the objection to immigrants: the problem is easily solved with the next generation if they are well educated and well integrated into American communities. And far from rejecting "American values" of hard work to provide a better life for themselves and their families, that is precisely the reason they have come here and go to extraordinary measures to stay. If a path to citizenship were available to them, most would take it.

In fact, from an economic point of view, the wave of immigrants, legal and undocumented (leaving aside, as always, criminals) has come at the very time in American history where Americans are unwilling or unable to do many kinds of hard and tedious labor. Of course, most of the illegal immigrants are contributing daily to the overall economy, and many of them impact our daily lives positively.

Assimilation

When the Irish, Italians and the Germans arrived in America in the 19th century, they had a difficult time becoming assimilated into American culture, but over time, they not only fit into American society but contributed greatly to its richness, diversity and economic power. Remarkably, we are hearing many of the same arguments now about the immigrants -- they can't speak English, they aren't educated, they resist assimilation.

A key to a successful immigration policy is providing pathways to assimilation, none of which are going to be built if the authorities are going to chase people down and deport them. Professor Jacob Vigor from Duke University has noted – "assimilation is the process of erasing difference between immigrants and natives over time. These differences are eroding just as rapidly now as they have historically." In other words, once assimilation is understood as a multi-generational process, the short-term criticisms about immigrants are muted.

In a study released in November 2011, demographers Dowell Myers and John Pitkin of the University of Southern California tracked advances that immigrants made who arrived in this country in the 1990's. The immigrants in the study were all over age 20. The authors, Messrs. Myers and Pitkin, concluded that these immigrants, who mainly came from Latin America and Asia, "made consistent progress towards social and economic integration until the recent recession."

They also found that only 24% of the immigrants who came here in the 1990's owned homes. They estimate that that figure will reach 72-percent by 2030. "Home ownership reflects the value immigrants place on achieving the American dream and the fact that they pool money to buy lower-priced real estate to achieve that dream," says Mr. Myers. "By 2030, 70% of all immigrants will speak English well, and 87-percent will be living above the government-defined poverty line," he predicts.

Mr. Vigdor of the Manhattan Institute found similarly processed trends for immigrants in his research. The latest study, a comparative analysis released in 2011, concluded that immigrants in the U.S. are more assimilated than in most European countries and only are less assimilated than those in Canada and Portugal.

This long-term positive assessment of immigrants, however, is difficult to sustain in the midst of a recession when there is high unemployment and considerable fear whether the entire economy of the world can be regarded with anything like stability. Nevertheless, these gains by immigrants, despite current policies, point to the possibilities if the policies encouraged assimilation.

It would be difficult to find many Americans who do not believe in and applaud entrepreneurship. Although some groups may begrudge success, this is typically as a result of misplaced jealousy and almost always only the case when it can be done with some level of anonymity. The Occupy Wall Street movement, as an example, fought (and still fights) against greed and corruption, not against the success of a business owner or even an individual employee. People who believe in the "ship'em out" approach to immigration do so under the veil of secrecy and anonymity. Many are quite engaged with and even fond of the person who brings them their hamburger at the local pub or restaurant, and they tend to be very pleased and even grateful for the good job their landscaper is doing. Exuding a certain level of pride in how capable and hard-working "these people" are. Surely, they reflect the spirit of the American Dream.

Few in America discourage entrepreneurship, to the contrary, most of us praise the spirit and hope for more job-creating entrepreneurs. As it pertains to the immigration debate, entrepreneurship plays a big part. How do we construct an enlightened immigration policy to make sure that a higher percentage of potential entrepreneurs stay in this country. A majority of the new jobs created in the U.S. economy come from new businesses, businesses that are less than five years old and that are started, by definition, by entrepreneurs. Many of these entrepreneurs, as has been detailed previously, are foreign-born U.S.-educated individuals. The point is that there is such free trade, and free flow of information that immigrants have the choice to start their businesses anywhere they wish. Should we and can we move forward, move past ideology and establish an economic incentive program that allows these foreign-born immigrants to start businesses here?

But some will argue that a prerequisite for being a successful business person is education. Okay. So let's work toward that, not only by keeping people who are already educated here and working, but building a foundation of education for the children of immigrants who are currently uneducated, so that they can be in a position that their children can become educated. Programs like the California Dream Act or the Ohio Dream Act are absolutely critical and that the next generation is that well-educated workforce that we need here in this country.

If we make sure that the current wave of immigrants are here safely, that their children participate in the school system and have an opportunity to be educated, they will quite naturally become assimilated. The research shows many immigrants are already pursuing the American dream. Why else are the pooling their monies to buy homes, which of course helps the hurting housing market. And with that taste of an even better life, surely many of their children, who are becoming much better educated than their parents, will turn out to be entrepreneurs, with greater incomes, more job creation and greater tax revenues.

By the way, you do not have to be a Ph.D. or have a postgraduate doctorate of any sort to become an entrepreneur. Both Bill Gates and Steve Jobs dropped out of graduate school in college. But with increased education the odds become better that people are going to be able to figure out how to make a better living because they possess the thinking skills that only education can produce.

CHAPTER 5

The cost of policy decisions:

It is simply wrong to say that immigrants are adding to our unemployment woes by taking jobs away from Americans. First of all, let us be clear about our word selection. Immigrants are here legally, with a visa; migrant workers are also here legally, on temporary visas (mostly in California) – so, often, when we talk about immigrants, we are really specifically referring to "illegal" immigrants. It is important to recognize that jobs illegal immigrants are taking are in most cases jobs Americans simply do not want. Whether it is the landscaping job, the busboy at your local restaurant, or the guy cleaning the turn-belts and brushes at the local carwash, the fact is that the vast majority of work done by illegal immigrants is work that most Americans won't do and view as beneath them.

However, research shows that there is some truth in the accusation that illegal immigrants negatively impact wages and in fact lower wages for Americans seeking similar jobs. During times of economic recession, while the economy is going through an "adjustment period," the added labor force does have a slight negative impact on both employment of Americans and average wages earned. It is important to note that this only holds true for the lowest skilled workers in America. The vast majority of Americans, who do not work as busboys, berry pickers or day laborers, are not negatively affected by immigration.

The Center for American Progress published a research study in early 2012 that takes a comprehensive look at the cost of our current immigration policy. Here are some facts from the report:

- In spite of nearly ten-folding the U.S. border patrols budget, illegal immigration to the Unites States has increased dramatically. The report cites that since 1992 – the year before our current enhanced detention and deportation policy began, the U.S. border patrols' budget has increased 714%.

- The current mass-deportation policy is reducing U.S. GDP by 1.46%, or $2.6 trillion over 10 years.

- The stronger enforcement policy has also created a sharp increase in human smuggling, which in turn increases violence and drug smuggling.

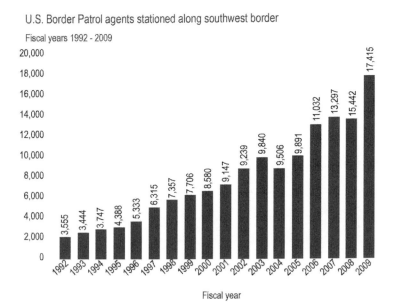

U.S. Border Patrol agents stationed along southwest border

Fiscal years 1992 - 2009

Fiscal year

Source: U.S. Border Patrol Headquarters, Office of Public Affairs (2009)

Alabama has learned first-hand the consequences of harsh anti-immigration laws. Since the State imposed the most severe law regarding immigrants in the nation, their economy has deteriorated further. Farmers simply do not have enough people to pick their crops and other solutions that involve traditional American citizens are not working. Just ask Guiseppe Peturis, an Alabama Farmer, who grows vegetables on is 20-acre farm in Belforest, Alabama Peturis, in a recent interview, stated that he was no fan of Republican Gov. Robert Bentley's plan to help unemployed citizens of the state find work. Governor Bentley passed the nation's toughest immigration law, requiring, among other things, police to detain suspects of being in the country illegally. This law has created a vacuum of farm work. Mr. Peturis has tried to hire through the state unemployment office, but without success. "Two of them left in 30 minutes; didn't even tell us they (were) going to leave," Peturis says. "One worked an hour and says it was too hard on his back."

As the Thanksgiving season approached in Alabama last year, so does strawberry planting season. In Baldwin County, on the Gulf Coast, farmers wondered if they will have the crews to get the plants in the ground. "We need help doing it and we need help that is going to come back every day," says Mark Krupinski, whose family farms about 900 acres in Foley, Alabama. He says the work is hard, and when local people ask him about a job, they want to drive a tractor, not work in the fields. "This isn't the kind of job most of us want to do," says Krupinski. "I don't blame them for not wanting to do (it), but somebody's got to do it if we're going to keep eating for the price that we are eating at."

There is another aspect of the draconian immigration policies of Alabama that I have to mention. If you're not sure just how severe they are, listen to Mickey Hammon, the Alabama legislator who co-authored the bill: "It attacks every aspect of an illegal immigrant's life. They will not stay in Alabama. This bill is designed to make it difficult for them to live here so they will deport themselves." So much for Southern hospitality.

A Faulty Premise and Alabama

Arizona, Alabama and some other states have passed harsh immigration laws, in large part on the premise that illegal immigrants are taking valuable jobs away from Americans. The evidence in Alabama points to the exact opposite. Elizabeth Dworkin wrote a provocative article on this subject.

She found that Americans do not want many of the jobs that illegal immigrants have. Once again, we wind up in Alabama. She writes, "In Alabama some 211,000 people are out of work, in rural Perry County, where Harvest Select is located, the unemployment rate is 18.2-percent, twice the national average. One of the big selling points of the immigration law is that it would free up jobs that Republican Governor Robert Bentley said immigrants had stolen from recession-battered Americans. Yet native Alabamians have not come running to fill these newly liberated positions. Many employers think the law is ludicrous and fought to stop it. Immigrants aren't stealing anything from anyone, they say. Businesses turned to foreign labor only because they couldn't find enough Americans to take the work they were offering. "At a moment when the country is relentlessly focused on unemployment, there are still jobs that often go unfilled. These are difficult, dirty, exhausting jobs that, for previous generations, were the first rickety step on the ladder to prosperity. They still are—just not for Americans."

I think this point is incredibly important because if you are going to argue that immigrants are stealing American jobs, then the question is where is the proof in that? The proof and the evidence are actually overwhelmingly in the other direction. The question is, would cracking down on illegal immigration make the US labor market much better off? There is significant evidence, as illustrated above, that reducing the number of illegal immigrants and migrant workers will actually harm our economy. Moreover, it will not just impact American businesses negatively, their absence will also eliminate the consumption of goods and services from immigrants. As Englishman John Tolland wrote in 1714, fifty years before the American Revolution, "The vulgar, I confess are seldom pleased in a country with the coming the foreigners. From their grudging at more persons sharing the same trades or business with them..." But Tolland also explained why this fear need not be realized: "We deny not that there will be more tailors and shoemakers; but there will also be more suits and shoes made for, and sold to the immigrants, amongst others." Lastly, for those who argue that deporting illegal immigrants will save states money in social services, the evidence on this is at best mixed. Most illegal immigrants take very little in forms of social services, as their lack of documentation makes the process almost impossible. The most costly of the programs, such as Social Security, Medicare and Medicaid, as well as unemployment benefits are far out of reach for illegal immigrants.

American workers by contrast are taking those benefits, not unreasonably. (This is surely a program that saves many a family from ruin, but it must act, at some level, as a disincentive to take some of those hard jobs that illegals are willing to do. Do not misunderstand: I'm always a believer in a bigger pie, not smaller slices).

I hate to keep picking on Alabama but nowhere in recent history is the folly of current practices more clear: farmer's losing income, crops languishing or wasted, tax revenue down, families uprooted, and root vegetables not uprooted. Most restaurants we all eat at would close tomorrow if there were the crackdown on illegals that some people want -- the same people who would be shocked at the price of a meal if citizens had those jobs, which they probably wouldn't take anyway. Or simply consider your own house and yard -- "we can't have all these non-citizens in these jobs." But we do we can and we must.

When children born in America have one parent that is a legal alien and the other illegal, the illegal one can be deported. And if the illegal one happens to be the main breadwinner, the ones left behind are thrown on social services for support thus increasing the expenditure of tax money. Similarly, when an immigrant is here legally in the United States and their spouse is abroad, the spouse cannot join his or her partner, even though they might be perusing legal entrance.

In the case of Lilliam Rodriguez, a sexton in a church in Greenwich CT, her husband was stranded in Costa Rica, working there, but unable to join his wife. She would occasionally go to see him but the whole arrangement was a great strain on their marriage. At some point, Lilliam received a letter from the INS. She opened it with excitement because she thought it was news that her husband had been granted permission to join her. Instead, it was an order to deport her meaning she would lose her job, her home, everything.

The church hired an immigration lawyer for their sexton, who they didn't want to lose. She and the lawyer discovered that the INS had sent a letter asking for some further documentation to the wrong address. Lilliam never knew the letter existed. For weeks, petitions were filed and letters were exchanged, while Lilliam waited anxiously, wondering about her fate and her family's. Finally, the INS acknowledged the mistake, and Lilliam tearfully thanked the church for their support. In time, her husband was able to join her and was hired as an additional sexton by the church. They now have a child together. And lest you think I have lost my way, they are both, of course, spending money on cars and diapers and food and rent. And paying taxes! But without the help of a generous church, they would have both been back in Costa Rica, struggling and shattered.

What about those spouses who are allowed to come here, but don't have work? Well, I would guess that even if the family was forbidden to collect additional benefits, which puts an added burden on the taxpayers, they would rather be united and looking for work than separated from their family.

The Obama administration is doing what it can to get rid of parts of the immigration laws that unnecessarily tear apart families. Citizenship and Immigration Services are proposing to change the procedures by which illegal immigrants with American family members apply for legal residency that is, allowing the crucial early step of getting a green card to take place in the US rather than in the immigrants' home country. If you put the politics of is aside, I suspect that the majority of you reading this book agree that developing a legal framework that reunites families is a sensible and "American" thing to do.

Immigration is unquestionably positive for a countries economy. However, the immigration topic, specifically illegal immigration is the biggest stumbling block to developing a cohesive, productive immigration policy. The fact is that 11.5 million illegal immigrants live in the United States, and over 86% of them have been here for more than 7 years. Many of them are part of our daily lives. We must develop a mechanism to allow them to remain here – the consequences of their departure would be economic ruin for US!

An alliance of 25 agricultural groups, led by Allie Devine a Republican and former Agriculture Secretary for the State of Kansas, has proposed Kansas House Bill #2712. The bill would allow illegal immigrants who have been in the United States for more than 5 years, are working, trying to learn English, paying taxes and have no criminal record to stay in the country legally with a path to citizenship. Bill Gordon, who supports the group, is the owner of signature landscape in Kansas. He has tried hiring Americans for his business, but has not been able to fill the job openings he has with Americans. He has run "Help Wanted" ads for the 2012 season with a starting wage of $8.63 per hour. He has 70 job openings, and the Kansas unemployment rate is well above 9%. He has had 7 applicants, 3 of whom showed up for the interview, and one of whom came to work – for 1 day. The fact is that Americans simply do not want these jobs. It's not a question of wages or job availability. It's a question of the type of work. Mr. Gordon wants to hire Americans, and is willing to "pay up" – but he can't; Americans just don't want these jobs.

The ship'em out argument:

To start off, given our overall fiscal strains, I suggest all of our politicians must take an 8th grade math course and pass it (I'm convinced the majority would fail a third grade test). I say this because of the ridiculous conclusion House Immigration Subcommittee Chairman Elton Gallegly (R-Calif.), Vice Chairman Steve King (R-Iowa) and Judiciary Committee Chairman Lamar Smith (R-Tex.) have come to. Mr. Gallegly, for one, has proposed deporting 11 million undocumented immigrants and their families. The basis for his argument is that these illegal immigrants are stealing American jobs. Even if this were the case, deporting 11 million people is impossible. Steve King has a slightly modified expectation. He is suggesting that by kicking out all illegal immigrants we would cut the unemployment rate in half or at least one third. Seriously, these guys are our leaders? I mean, just consider this: Illegal immigrants are not part of the official workforce, so they are not even calculated in the 14, 15, 16 million unemployed or underemployed people in America.

People who oppose immigration reform, like Kansas Secretary of State Chris Koback, point to the opinion that if businesses would raise the wages they pay, plenty of Americans would take the jobs offered. He is a law professor and one of the architects of the Arizona Immigration law. When asked about immigration and the impact the absence of illegal immigrants would have on businesses, Mr. Koback insists that "market forces" would prevail and would drive Americans to accept these jobs – if the wages are high enough. Of course, his argument regarding the impact on competitiveness for various industries lacks any foundation in economic realities. He argues that even industries like agriculture would not suffer if all business in the agricultural field were forced to pay higher wages. Putting aside the fact that few would be willing to pay $10 for a bushel of grapes, he is also ignoring the impact of foreign competition. I'm all for buying American, but not at any price. If you believe, as I do, that business people, not bureaucrats or politicians have the best sense of how their business operates, then we should listen to our farmers, builders, restaurateurs and other business leaders.

As previously discussed, in the long-run immigration has a very positive effect on our economy. Take the State of California for instance. California has one of the highest populations of immigrants and illegal immigrants in the United States. According to a study done by the nonpartisan Migration Policy Institute in 2011, "California, where the share of immigrants in employment increased from 25% in 1990 to 35% in 2007, the average income per worker increased by 2.6 % in real terms over that period. There were similar gains in income per worker in Texas (where the share of immigrant employment grew from 11% to 21% between 1990 and 2007) or in New York, where immigrant employment grew from 18% to 27%."

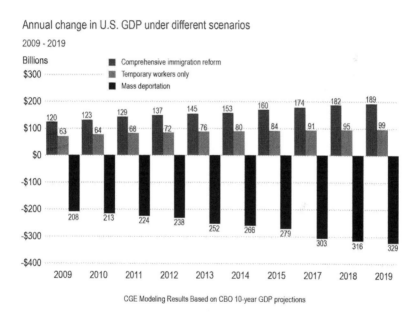

Annual change in U.S. GDP under different scenarios

2009 - 2019

CGE Modeling Results Based on CBO 10-year GDP projections

According to the Migration Policy Institute, illegal immigrants often create the jobs they work in. As a result of the contribution to the American economy illegal immigrants make, additional jobs are created and with these jobs come additional goods and services. The simple economic reality is that illegal immigrants, just like any other employed individual in any country, contribute to an economy by consuming and buying goods. They make the economy bigger, in turn increasing the demand for labor. When illegal immigrants build homes, make burgers, bus tables in restaurants and to do all the things that they do, they also go out and consume goods. This additional consumption adds nearly $20 billion of economic activity to our economy each year. Even the least educated and lowest paid immigrants are part of this equation. The addition of low-skilled immigrant workers expands the overall size of the economy. It creates a higher wage opening because migrants spend, build and create, even at the most menial task.

From a purely economic perspective, immigration has great benefits to the United States. As a matter of fact, the CATO Institute's study said that legalizing low-skilled immigrant workers would add some $180 billion to U.S. GDP over the next 10 years. That is a significant sum. By the way, if we were to kick out all of the illegal immigrants, in particular the migrant workers, we'd probably end up paying somewhere between $12 and $15 for a pint of blueberries, even if the blueberries ever got picked in the first place. I do not know about you, but I am not willing to do that. The math is pretty simple on this one.

The Criminal Element:

Let us also examine the idea that immigration inevitably, always leads to criminal activity. And let's not define criminal activity as simply migrating from one place on the planet to another in the search of a better future, but let's define it as actual crimes for which you or I as readers, if we were to do them, would go to jail for or be punished in some way. I think this misunderstanding of the facts was one of the reasons that the Arizona Governor Jan Brewer listed for the incredibly harsh crackdown on illegal immigration that she pursued and supported as part of the State's Immigration Reform.

Now, if she had gone to Nogales, one of Arizona's cities that straddle the Mexican border Mexico most directly, she would have discovered a very unpleasant truth. In 2000, Nogales experienced 23 rapes, robberies and murders. In 2009 after 10 years of population growth—which was mostly fueled by illegal immigration—we are talking on the U.S. side—there were 19 such crimes. Aggravated assaults dropped by one third, and there have been no murders for more than two years. So much for immigration driven crime waves.

I recognize that certain people in the media may dismiss this as a single example, but the facts are the facts are the facts. There have been some substantial studies done on this aspect of immigration.

Tim Wadsworth of the University of Colorado, who is a sociology professor, did some research on crime and immigration and has debunked the notion that more immigration necessarily equals more crime. I am not saying that no immigrants are criminals. I am simply saying that no greater a percentage of immigrants are criminals than non-immigrants, than legal citizens. It is true that by default, all illegal immigrants have broken the law in the sense that they have come here, but we need to look at it again differently.

What Professor Wadsworth worked with statistics from the 1990's. He found that cities that attracted more immigrants, cities like Los Angeles, San Francisco, San Diego, in the State of California, experienced falls in homicide and robbery. The same cities that saw the most foreign immigration in the 1990's were also the leaders in the next 10 years and in most of them, violent crime continued to trend down. Wadsworth did not stop at big cities. He looked at over 459 communities with populations of at least 50,000 people. He distinguished the effects of legal and illegal immigration as best as he could by using U.S. census reports, which has difficulties but is not impossible.

What he noticed was that immigrant citizens and non-citizens often congregated in the same areas for reasons of culture and language, an expected result of the impulse for assimilation. He tracked robberies and homicides because they are harder to hide than other crimes. "Rather than causing crime waves," Wadsworth says, "the numbers suggest that integration may be partially responsible for the decrease in violent crime." His statistical analysis shows that the growth in the new immigrant population, on average in the 459 cities that he visited, led to a near 10-percent decline in the murder rate and a 22% decline in robberies.

What's puzzling about his results is that they are so at odds with the statistics Arizona relies on. In 2010 illegal immigrants made up about 7% of Arizona's population, but they represented roughly 15% of the prison population. They represented 14% of those held on manslaughter and 24% of those held on drug charges. The reality is that despite the decrease in the overall crime rate a disproportionate number of illegal immigrants are incarcerated for serious crimes. True, poor immigrants have a much higher likelihood of being incarcerated but is that because they are committing more crimes? Arizona's numbers seem to be an anomaly.

About all anyone can say, I think, is that there is no conclusive evidence that links immigration to increased crime. And if that is true -- and if the best unbiased studies actually support the fact that crime drops with increased immigration, then a popular argument that has worked its way into the immigration debate is removed and we will base our policies on facts rather than unfounded assumptions.

These humanitarian considerations are not tangential to a sound immigration policy. Governments like stable families as much as the stable families themselves. But the foundation of the immigration solution must be economic. By seriously analyzing America's skill and employment needs at all levels, we then have the chance to begin matching the number and types of immigrants we need. When I say "types" I do not mean -- and I positively reject -- racial or ethnic profiling. If we go down that road, we will wind up ignoring smart people eager to succeed. No, what I mean is that skill sets that match the employment demands will result in a more productive, creative and energetic work force that can help fuel our economy.

The solution to the "immigration problem" is not to throw them out. It is invite them in, deliberately and intelligently.

CHAPTER 6

The underground economy

The so called "underground" economy -- or getting paid off the books -- is a phenomenon at least as old as Robin Hood. Most economists agree that the underground economy in the United States represents between 8% and 10% of GDP or between $1.15 trillion and $1.45 trillion dollars per year. Economist Edgar Feige estimated that in 2009, the U.S> government missed out on over $600 billion in tax revenues as a result of the existence of the underground economy. This figure has grown in recent years, predominantly as a result of the economic crisis of 2007 and 2008 and the ensuing recession. When people lose their jobs or become underemployed (wages being cut), they enter the underground, or "informal" economy. The underground economy is not just comprised or maids, landscapers or day-worker getting paid off the books. It is also comprised of work for barter – exchanging one set of skills for another.

Participation in the underground economy comes from both employees and employers, often both working deliberately together to avoid taxes. As the cost of taxes and social security become a greater burden on business – which is most prevalent during hard economic times – the informal or underground economy expands. Although illegal immigrants do participate in the underground economy, their role is relatively small compared to the other components.

The reality, however, is that the majority of undocumented workers in the United States work with a false social security number, paying taxes – in part, for benefits they will never use. As the United States continues to experience high unemployment rates and significant underemployment rates, our citizens – natural born US citizens – are gravitating to the underground economy. This goes well beyond the homeless collecting aluminum cans or day laborers waiting outside the local Home Depot. It includes the working poor holding yard-sales, selling personal belongings on Ebay, inflating the value of donations to charities (in same cases just making them up), and of course underreporting tips and gratuities. The reality is, that virtually all Americans are participating in the underground economy to one extent or another.

Alfonso Morales, a professor at the University of Wisconsin has studied the impact of the underground economy extensively and has concluded that all-in-all, the existence of the underground economy is "probably neutral to good", since "people who make their money in unregulated businesses probably spend it in regulated ones." As Columbia University professor Saskia Sassen points out in her book *Cities in a World Economy,* the underground economy does not just consist of low-wage low-skilled workers, but also of highly educated and skilled people. "In brief, the new informal economy in global cities is part of advanced capitalism. One way of putting it is that the new type of informalization of work are the low-cost equivalent of formal deregulation in finance, telecommunications and most other economic sectors in the name of flexibility and innovation. The difference is that while formal deregulation was costly, and tax revenue as well as private capital went into paying for it, informalization is low-cost and largely on the backs of the workers and firms themselves."

There is however, a large problem associated with the underground economy. According to a report by the Federal Deposit Insurance Corporation, as of the end of 2009 some 7.7 % of U.S. households don't have bank accounts. And roughly 21 million people are "under-banked" meaning that they use cash only or use other sources -- Western Union, say -- to transmit payments. A significant portion of people using these "alternative" banking methods are immigrants, costing tax payers significant lost revenues. All of this cash floating around is under-taxed, and we as a society are paying for it.

Every time we write out a check to "cash" for a service done, we participate in it, we insure that the amount of tax dollars available for services is diminished. Businesses that run their entire operation more or less on this model (Cash Only! the sign says) are perhaps particularly guilty of robbing the public coffers. There is a school of thought -- the ability of human beings to acquit themselves is practically endless -- that since the government would probably waste the money anyway or spend it on people who have no real right to it, the secreting of the cash is actually morally justified. Of course, we need look no further than Greece and the current sovereign debt crisis to see where that thinking leads. Nobody likes taxes, but economies depend on them.

Many people who realize the necessity of taxes for a stable society and pay their fair share believe that immigrants, both legal and illegal, are especially blameworthy participants in the underground economy, which amounts to some $10 billion a year by some estimates (or roughly half of the interest earned on the Wall Street bailouts in 2011). Now it is true that illegal immigrants, who have very little standing in the society, sometimes have to go underground because the nature of their jobs are usually of the cash variety. But the real problem is that even if the system encouraged them to pay taxes -- and keep in mind illegal aliens do pay more than $4200 a year on average -- the kinds of jobs they can get, given their lack of education, produce low wages and therefore low or no taxes. In fact, most illegal immigrants who have payroll taxes deducted from their checks would qualify for a refund under our existing tax code. However, because the social security number is fraudulent or lacks back up information, no refund can be issued.

Immigration has varying impacts on various states. Some benefit more than other, some pay more per immigrant than others, but all benefit. There is not a single state that can claim that immigrants do not add to their GDP. From a cost perspective, California,

New York, New Jersey, Texas, Florida and Illinois "pay" the most per immigrant. California pays roughly $1178 per year in state and local services to illegal immigrant households. Costs in other states are lower, but still significant. However, when taking into account the economic benefit immigrants bring, the $1,178 per year is a smart investment.

For example, legal and illegal immigrants alike get health treatment (one hesitates to call it health care) at expensive emergency rooms through policies for the uninsured that amounts to about 2.2 billion a year. Their children benefit from a free school lunch program at a cost of 1.9 billion. And many of them receive food stamps. Hardliners might want to reverse all or some of this illusory largess, but as a society we have decided to face the fact that these human beings deserve some level of help when they are sick or need to eat. And it all amounts to much less than most people would guess.

In fact, on average, the cost of illegal households impose on the federal government is less than half that of other households. True, the taxes they pay are only one-fourth of other households, but we must ask why that is: low paying jobs, a system that discourages identification and a lack of education that might lead to higher paying jobs. For all of these "give-aways" however, the cost to the taxpayer is still significantly less than those created by other households, less in fact than legal immigrants. Merely giving illegals legal status would do nothing to reduce the cost burden.

Steven Camarota, Director of Research at the Center of Immigration Studies in Washington D.C. has convincingly shown that merely making them legal would actually cost the federal government more, not less. So what are we to do? Clearly, the current policies and proposed "solutions" are not working.

There are three possible policy alternatives. We can enforce the current (or stricter) immigration laws, reduce costs associated with immigrants or grant some kind of amnesty to illegals in order to raise tax revenues.

The first is being tried to disastrous effect by the State of Alabama at huge cost to the taxpayer, that is, probably an increase on the $2.75 billion now spent on detention and deportation. Since the children of illegal immigrants born in the United States are citizens, there is the added problem of what to do with them. Undoubtedly, some will leave and return to their country of origin with their parents, though I suspect, most will remain here. After all, the principal reason their parents illegally entered the United States was to provide a better life for their children. Most states already have an over-burdened child services and foster system. Adding several million more children could quickly break the system and is guaranteed to cost tax payers enormously. There is the long-term cost as well. You don't need to have a degree in psychology to recognize that the cost to children who arrive home to find their parents gone is incalculable. If we as a society were to really want to eradicate illegal and undocumented workers the cost would be, what, $10 billion? 12 billion? Don't forget to factor in all those unpicked crops, which would amount to millions of acres of food gone to waste or eventually, not planted at all. Besides, most illegal immigrants have families. Are we as a society willing to hound and separate families who are already well integrated into communities here? Isn't there a better way? There must be.

The second alternative is to reduce costs associated with immigrants: cut their food stamps, bar their children from school lunch programs, turn them away from hospitals when they are hurting. Putting aside the Nazi-like state we would need to create to ensure everyone has proper documentation, this is not only an unrealistic solution, but also a economically damaging one. Those who are advocates of this type of policy are speaking emotionally and have not thought through the implementation process. How would you react, if your dark haired son or daughter, with a dark summer tan, where detained and kept from going to school because "he or she looks foreign" and doesn't have proper identification with them. Even if you could tell which immigrants are legal or illegal -- not an easy task -- are we prepared to carry around a raft of papers proving that we are one of the "allowed" ones. Since I frequently carry my insurance card in my brief case, which I don't always have by my side, I would hate to be crushed in a car accident, only to be turned away at the doors of the emergency room because I lack proper identification. Harsh measures -- even if they are for those "other people" have consequences for the kind of society we want to be.

Besides, just from a purely economic point of view, we wouldn't save all that much since illegal households impose only about 46 percent of the cost to the federal government compared to legal households.

Well, what if we provided some sort of path of amnesty? Would tax revenues go up? In short, yes. But then costs would go up too. Why? Because the underlying factors wouldn't change: low levels of education that lead to hard labor job that don't pay very much, yielding low tax revenues. The fact is that most illegal immigrants, even if you declared them legal, would remain relatively poor.

The simple reality is that without governmental leadership in this area, including immigration and economic reform, people will continue to find ways to navigate these rough economic times. Worse, once they become entrenched in the informal economy, they become comfortable with it and are likely to continue to exist within it. As Professor Saskian points out "people shouldn't have to give up fundamental human rights like access to income in retirement or safety on the job because they need work." But, in an economy that tolerates increasing levels of income disparity and high levels of unemployment, the underground economy is often the only alternative to starvation.

CHAPTER 7

The Great Brain Drain

Education Matters

If we are serious about reforming our immigration policy, we must also address our crumbling education system. This requires a two-pronged approach to education.

First, we cannot allow one generation of immigrants stuck in low wage jobs to continue into the next. If we provide their children education, it may prove expensive in the short run. That's because it requires all of the services of a school (building, teachers, playing fields etc…) plus additional services such as school lunches and food stamps. But the result is and will be a society that reaps benefits for years to come. This opportunity needs to be viewed as an investment in our future, rather than an expense. The color of a child's skin or their native tongue should not determine whether or not we help those children and foster their growth. This investment, will pay hefty dividends in just a few short years, and will carry a great cost to our society if it is not made. By encouraging children to learn and become successful, we as a nation will win. It may not look like the America of the 1950's, but then again, it already doesn't. We need to teach our youth the right skills and knowledge, so that they too can share in the American dream.

This accords with what the immigrants themselves have demonstrated throughout our history. Second generation immigrants are more likely to have a high school degree than their parents compared to their citizen counterparts. This is a critical component to assimilation, integration and ultimately to higher levels of tax revenues.

The second component needs to address the "Brain Drain" that is occurring in this country. The millions of highly educated young men and women who attend our universities and are then forced to leave our county – because their student visas run out.

Number of Patents Granted per 10,000 Post-College Graduates

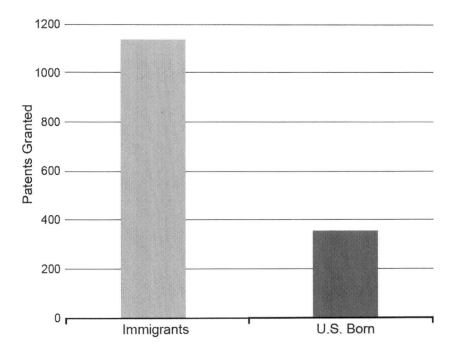

Source: Patents granted over the period 1998-2003. Hunt and Gauthier-Loiselle (2003), Table 1

Foreign students, who make up about 20% of our university student bodies in the United States, received nearly half of all the science, engineering, mathematics and economics degrees received in 2010. We, America, need these skills and these immigrants. We are actively rejecting and throwing out these highly desirable workers.

We need to understand that once these people leave, they are usually gone forever, and with what goes with them are the jobs that they would create here in the United States.

If the brain drain in the United States were to be addressed, it would mean immediate impact on our fiscal situation. With roughly 3.6 million engineering, science and other high paying jobs going unfilled because appropriately skilled people are not available, the best solution is to import those skills, starting with the "imported" people who are already here.

The various levels of visa programs that exist to address this problem should be expanded so that the default on visas is not that they run out but that they offer these skilled graduates of our universities a reason to stay. For if they were given preferential treatment over other immigrants who are looking for jobs, the incentive would be considerable.

I will absolutely endorse the argument that if there is an American citizen who is qualified and able to get the job and that person is competing with a non-American citizen and they truly are equal in skills, then the preference should go to the American citizen. Most countries do favor natives. Sadly, in America today, the skills gap is too great to have this occur on a frequent basis. The 3.6 million science, engineering and mathematics based jobs available are going unfilled because there are not enough engineers and scientists available. The vacancies are not because we do not have any unemployment in the country, but because the supply of labor and the demand for labor are not matched up properly.

Let's talk about another kind of immigrant student, not one that wants to be hired by a company, but a true entrepreneur who wants to start one and hire employs. That dream might start in college and be furthered though contacts with other students who have established contacts in this country. But if such students know that their visa is going to expire a few days after graduation, it makes for a very different mind-set for these ambitious people. They will likely take all their education and good ideas back to their home country, which wins big in this foolish policy we are perusing. It goes without saying that all of us lose.

That kind of education reform will mean that over the next 15 to 20 years we will have a self-sustaining system in which our boys and girls are graduating from high school or graduating from college with the right degree and the right education. They do not all have to be scientists, but we need to step up our game and we need to increase the effectiveness of the type of education that we provide our children.

If only half of the roughly 250,000 foreign students remained in the country each year, got jobs, and started paying taxes, our balance sheet would quickly start showing signs of improvements. By my estimates, after 10 years of this policy, the United States would benefit from an additional 2 million tax payers, generating over $400 million in additional tax revenues, and adding over $2 billion in additional consumption (GDP) to our country.

There are not enough Green-Cards

Just to be clear, the current policy is this: the immigration law strictly limits the number of Green Cards that can be awarded to each nation. Countries are limited to receive 7% of 140,000 green cards (ergo, 9,800) no matter the size of the countries' population or the quality of their applicants. In other words, China or India will receive the same number of Green Cards as Greece or Belgium – both of which have a population that is roughly 1% of China's.

Contemplate this. Right now, there are about 210,000 Indian professionals in line for this green card, meaning that only the most persistent and lucky of them won't have a 70 year wait. The Chinese applicants are facing a 20 year wait. These are people who want to be here, to work here, to pay taxes here. How does this policy make sense?

It doesn't especially if you consider the case of Amit Aharoni, an Israeli national who graduated from the Stanford Business School. He secured $1.65 million in venture capital to start a business, along with two other of his college graduates, called Cruisewise.com. The company hired nine Americans in just one year.

But Aharoni ran up against the U.S. Citizenship and Immigration Services in October of 2011 when they denied his request for a visa and directed him to leave the country immediately. He did. He moved to Canada. He's currently paying taxes there.

The Wharton School of Business produced a paper called Brain Drain or Brain Exchange, What is the Cost When Immigrant Entrepreneurs Go Home. In it, it tells the story of Vivek Wadhwa who came to the United States in 1980 and started two companies that created 1,000 American jobs. Wadhwa, who now teaches at Duke University, has been doing a lot of thinking about this conundrum. He has come up with a novel, but eminently sensible idea that has gotten as far as Congress: fast track immigrant graduates. Even if they don't start a business -- and many of them will -- they are precisely the kind of people our society needs. If they do start a business, it will mean hundreds maybe thousands of jobs in the short term and hundreds of thousands in the longer term.

Of course, even with this provision, many may return home. Okay, but at the moment almost all of them are required to whether they want to or not. Let's not underestimate the competition. The rest of the world is catching up rapidly. Chili, for example offers a permanent visa and $30,000 in startup capital, plus free rent to tech entrepreneurs willing to take their business there. Nevertheless, America is still the place to be if you're hoping for venture capital and other incentives to start a business.

All of this would be bad enough, but it gets worse. Not only do we send skilled people away, we lock them up.

Education vs. Incarceration

Since 2000, the State of California has built nine new prisons and only one new college campus. That says a lot about the priorities and the influence of lobbyists on our nations policies. I hazard a guess to say that few Americans think that we should build more prisons and fewer schools, that incarceration is more important than educating our youth. Yet, that is the state of our nation. The U.S. prison system is costing US tax payers just over $50 billion per year. By way of comparison, the fiscal 2011 budget for the US department of Education was $31 billion. Soon we will be spending twice as much on incarceration than we will on education.

The American dream is a simple and wonderful thing and I believe it is the dream of people around the world regardless of where they come from or live. Simply put, we all want the same thing. We want a home. We want a job. We want respect. We want to be treated with dignity and we want to ensure that our children are better off than we are. That is the American dream. So the question is, when somebody comes into the United States and does nothing wrong other than coming here illegally, should that person really be incarcerated and should that person be incarcerated at a cost of nearly $2 billion a week to taxpayers. That, to me, is insane.

In 2008, the United States had about 1.3 million college graduates (graduating in 2008). China and India, by way of comparison, had 3.3 million and 3.1 million students graduating from their universities – almost all of them staying in their respective countries, paying taxes and increasing GDP. Most significantly, over the past decades, China's and India's education budgets have grown by more than ten-fold, while ours has stayed stagnant. What's even more astounding is that virtually all of the graduating students in China and India speak English fluently – can you spell competitive advantage?

As of the end of 2011, there are roughly 2.3 million people behind bars in the United States. That, by the way, is more than the population of the city of Houston, Texas, which is our country's fourth largest city and represents roughly 5% of the world's entire prison population. It costs us more than a billion dollars every week to have those 2.3 million behind a bar and it is absolutely crazy. No other nation on the planet, including China or India has a higher proportion or a higher absolute number of people in their prisons. The reality is, we simply incarcerate too many people.

When you think about the fact that we have 14 million illegal and undocumented immigrants in the country, you just cannot add them to that prison population. That is just not a viable solution.

Higher levels of education clearly affect the level of incarceration. There is plenty of evidence that the more educated somebody is, the less likely they are going to go to prison. So we do have to work on education for many reasons, but helping to keep people out of prison is one of them, if only for economic reasons. Reform should include educating the children of immigrants, whether they are here legally or illegally, and should incorporate things such as the California and Ohio Dream Act that allows these kids to go to college if they earn it and get financial assistance to do so. Any which way you do the math it makes sense and is beneficial for the long-term well-being of our nation. At the moment, some school districts will educate illegal immigrants but once they graduate, there is no chance for them to go on to college even if they want to -- and most do -- because they do not have the required social security number.

It is no secret that higher education leads to higher incomes. Of course, there is always the exception, but generally speaking, I think we can all agree that the more educated somebody is, the more likely they are to get a higher paying job. That is one of the issues our country faces.

As of 2008, roughly 20% of our children were in what is considered poverty. That is the highest percentage of all industrialized countries. By comparison, the lowest is Finland, which just has 4-percent of its children living below the line of poverty. That needs to be addressed with a long-term solution because there is no quick fix. The solution lies in education and we need to recognize that education must incorporate the education of the children of immigrants. We should move away from policies that are being discussed in states like Arizona and Alabama, where the discussion focuses on police and school officials having to check whether a child is here legally, or the parents are here legally. I understand that pundits will preach all day long that all politics are local, and that they will argue that the same could or should be said about our local schools. But there are some very real national themes involved in how we are approaching education.

To illustrate the difference this kind of planning can make consider, China and India both of which began their impressive rise in the world about 20 years ago. The first thing they did was they really invested in their education system and became aggressive in trying to send their brightest young minds abroad to study in Europe and predominately the United states. What that has resulted in is in 2010, the United States had roughly 1.3 million college graduates. By comparison, in the same year, India had 3.1 million college graduates and China had 3.3 million young men and women graduating from college that year. That is a big, big difference. That means some dire consequences for our economy and our way of life and we need to fix it.

India's budget for higher education for 2010 to 2015 is nine times higher than over the prior five years. By contrast, ours is stagnating. Anyone who is concerned with the direction our country is going, who wants to fix poverty, our social security system, our Medicare and Medicaid system, is concerned with homeland security and wants to put our nation back "on the right track." needs to understand that immigration and education are at the root of our woes and present the solution.

Young immigrants can be part of the solution

Our current demographics and resulting increasing need for government services such as Social Security and Elder Care require us to rethink and retool our entire approach to immigration. Purely economically speaking, the only viable long-term solution is for the United States to grow its way out of our current problems. We can debate tax cuts and government waste as long as we like, but at the end of it, we need to spend less per person and raise more revenues overall. In essence, what the facts demand is that we need to import people. Based on our current demographics and population trends, we need to add nearly 50 million young, productive people to our population over the next 20 years.

Ideally, the United States would "import" a mix of highly skilled labor as well as inexpensive manual labor – believe it or not, we will need more manual labor as our nations' population grows. Of course, we also need highly skilled and educated people who will be very productive members of our society, who will have high incomes, create jobs, increase productivity, and, of course, generate additional tax revenues. It is critical that we develop a long term perspective and plan that not only addresses our current needs, but looks ahead to the needs of the next generation and beyond. We need engineers, scientists, economists and mathematicians, the people we are unfortunately sending back to their home countries when they graduate from our fine universities and colleges.

A well thought out strategy that requires the "import" of immigrants to satisfy and meet our current economic and tax goals also requires that we think about our natural born population to ensure their success. While we need immigrants now, if we are deliberate in our reforms, we will take the steps necessary to ensure that our young boys and girls who are entering kindergarten, grade, middle and high school right now are being prepared with the right education to fill the jobs of tomorrow, so that at some point, we can stop importing immigrants. On a long-term basis, we can and must develop policies that allow the U.S. economy to be self-sustaining, and does not require aggressive immigration goals to meet its economic objectives. The "stop-gap" solution I am proposing is needed because we have not thought far enough ahead, and our current policies are failing us. Ideally speaking, this is a bridge that is designed to serve our purpose until we have enough people—American citizens—who can generate the tax revenues necessary to fix our economic woes.

The need for high skilled labor and sophistication of our society, however, does not eliminate the need for manual labor. Increasing skilled labor pools does not, by definition, impact the demand for low-skill, low-wage labor. The future, no matter how sophisticated, efficient and how much it relies on high skill labor will also require a large amount of cheap manual labor.

The Skills Gap

H-1B visas are geared towards highly skilled, highly qualified foreigners, many of them engineers and mathematicians. In order to qualify for a H-1B visa, applicants must have a Bachelors' Degree or equivalent (with the exception of models – pretty people get a break here too). In 2003, the cap for H-1B visas was 195,000, since 2005 the annual cap has stood at 85,000 – and I'll say it again: 3.6 million engineering and science jobs go unfilled. In 2008, the cap was filled in just 1 day. We are actively turning away entrepreneurs, scientists and leaders. This is the one part that we are getting right. The H-1B visas are split into two categories – academic or research institution, and private businesses. This is critical, as the makeup of the H-1B visas granted changes with our actual economic need. Sadly, and harmfully, the cap is currently set at a total of 85,000 for any calendar year.

There are some exceptions to the cap, but they are increasingly rare.

Over the last decade the demand for H-1B visas has fluctuated in response to both economic and political conditions. Most of the fluctuation in demand comes from capped requests, which ebb and flow with the business cycle, while demand from uncapped employers has remained steadier.

According to a report issued by The Brookings Institute, 50% of all H-1B visas are issued for computer experts. There are over 150,000 IT-related employees working in the United States under the H-1B visa system. The second most thought after group are engineers, who make up approximately 8.6% of recipients, followed by financial exports – many of them accountants and actuaries, who comprise 6.2% of visa recipients. The Medical profession also receives a significant amount of the visas', nearing 6% of grants.

High-Skill Immigration

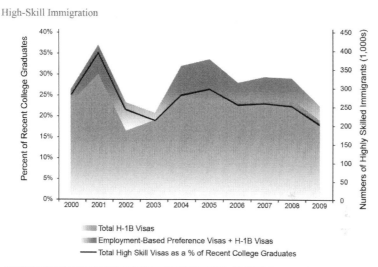

Note: Includes workers seeking legal permanent residence under Employment First (Eb-1), Second (Eb-2) and Third (Eb-3) Preference, new arrivals and adjustments, and H-1b Initial and Continuing Applications. College graduates refers to bacjelors degrees, and excludes bachelors conferred to non-resident aliens; Source: (2000-2009), NCES (2009)

Consider the State of Connecticut, my home state. In hospitals across the state, there is a need for qualified nurses and doctors. In particular, take Danbury Hospital, in Danbury CT. Like many hospitals in our nation, Danbury Hospital is a community hospital that tends to heart-attacks, babies' earaches, teenagers' broken limbs, and other common medical woes. Additionally, it is also a teaching hospital. Unfortunately, for the community and the hospital, in spite of significant investments in property and equipment, Danbury Hospital has not been able to attract enough applicants for its program. Andrea Rynn, a spokes-women for Western Connecticut

81

Health Network, which manages Danbury Hospital among others, recently explained "there aren't enough young doctors available for residency programs. There are very specific specialties – for example, primary care – where this is happening." As a result, of the shortage, and the growing need for care by the community, Danbury Hospital is going abroad to find qualified doctors and nurses. It is utilizing the governments' H-1B visa program. Recipients of the visa are allowed to work in the United States for three to six years. And with this time restrictions, begin the problems. It takes a lot of money and time to train highly skilled workers like doctors and nurses. Our current system invites them in to be trained, but then ejects them once they begin reaching their potential. The H-1B visa program is relied upon by some of America's greatest technology companies. Intel, IBM, Oracle, and Google request more H1-1B visas' than any other companies in the United States. There are also large foreign based companies that are requesting H-1B visas for their U.S. based operations. That's right, foreign companies coming to the United States to do business are not finding enough qualified and skilled workers in our country, and are importing them. As a tax payer, do you really believe that we should be spending nearly twice as much on prisons as we are on educating our youth? I sure the heck don't!

The challenge for policymakers is to figure out how to meet the demand for high-skilled workers by developing an immigration policy that allows the United States to continue to attract the foreign workers that it needs, while at the same time educating and training U.S. workers for these jobs in the near future. A pragmatic solution to America's skills needs calls for significant reforms in the H-1B visa program:

> We should create an independent "Standing Commission on Labor and Immigration" that will recommend to Congress timely changes to U.S. immigration policy in order to more nimbly respond to economic needs, including the demand for high-skilled foreign workers in regional labor markets – as you will see later, this information is readily available and published monthly.

> ➤ Go where the jobs are: Base the visas on our economic needs, and make sure to discriminate – geographically that is. We should target H-1B visa fees to metropolitan areas with a high demand for H-1B workers to train the existing workforce for high-demand skills needs. This is both sensible and will increase visa revenues. (I liken it to real estate taxes, different states and towns have varying tax levels, a similar difference can be applied to visa costs and fees).

Revamping our Tax System:

So far, we have approached the immigration topic from the perspective of what to do with or how to deal with our immigrants. There is of course a flip side to this – how do we avoid our tax paying base from leaving and immigrating to other nations. One extreme example of course is Facebook co-founder Eduardo Saverin, who recently renounced his U.S. citizenship to avoid paying taxes on the $2 billion plus he received when the company became public. We now live in a world where migration, in particular for the educated and wealthy, is easy. Attempts to eliminate social services for the wealthy and / or sharply increase taxes on the wealthy will simply provide further incentives to leave and move to a nation with a more favorable tax code. Companies, of course, have been doing this for years – it's called out-sourcing. Instead of building a new factory, call center or research facility in the United States, many companies have chosen to build them abroad – in Asia, Africa, the Middle-East, all will lower costs relating to taxes, insurance and social services. General Electric for instance, recently closed its Radiology plan in the United States and has moved it, along with several hundred high paying jobs, to India. GE management cites a lack of qualified labor, and cost (read tax) savings as a principal reason for the move. Of course there are other reasons, but financial cost is certainly one of the main drivers behind the decision. This is precisely why we need to incorporate tax reform as part of the debate. It is asking a lot, but will prove to be well worth the effort.

CHAPTER 8

Unemployment and the labor market

The worst of the economic crisis that began in 2007 is likely behind us. However, America's labor market continues to be strained and there are entirely too many unemployed Americans.

Given the current political climate, high levels of unemployment and overall malaise of our economy, it is understandable why many seek to find answers and place blame for their woes. With 14 million unemployed, there are 3.2 million jobs that go begging. Why? Because the supply of labor does not match the demand for labor. The job openings are relatively high paying manufacturing, engineering and science-based jobs, and there are not enough Americans to fill them.

As a result, we must raise the number of L1 visas that are issued – L1 visas are short-term visas that allow employees of international companies with offices in the United States to work in the U.S. for up to three years.

Over the past 20 years or so, both in the academic world and within the business community, the consensus has become that in the long-run, illegal immigration and immigration as a whole does not negatively affect employment of the US population. To the contrary, immigration creates jobs.

The current high levels in unemployment are as a result of a disconnect between labor demand and labor skills available – in short, as a people need to be retrained and educated to fill the jobs that are available. There has to be a balance of supply and demand in the structure of the business, industry and national economy for it all to work with something like efficiency. Okay, so in any given time period a lack of supply can spur some entrepreneur to take up the slack to his gain. But that is a far different circumstance from when a country, such as ours, lacks some 3.2 million highly skilled, high-paying and highly taxable jobs that go wanting. Who cannot see that every year those jobs are empty, the productivity they would have otherwise generated simply does not take place, and we fall farther behind in the global economy.

The solution: We as a country need to determine what labor needs we have, forecast what we are most likely to need in the next decade and beyond. We must develop a process that not only identifies our short-term needs, but also our long-term needs. The information is at our fingertips, we just have to have the courage to use the data. The way to get started is to implement a process that identifies and addresses our short-term needs. What type of jobs to we need to fill in the next 12, 24, and 36 months? I believe that if we can successfully demonstrate that a proactive immigration policy can benefit our economy and can help lift us from the challenging environment we are currently in, than we can develop a national policy that is geared to matching those needs over the long-term. Of course, that means strengthening the educational system here that is currently failing to produce anything like enough skilled people, especially at the top echelons. While we have had this discussion for a long time, we've made little to no progress on this critical issue.

So that means we are going to have to identify those people who graduate from our university in fields and with skills we need and make sure they stay here. Further, we may well need to search the world for those people who have the right skill sets for our labor market and incentivize them to come here. This will by no means strip countries of their brightest and best because few are willing to pick up from their home land and culture and come here. But some will.

Consider what would then follow. A recent study by Stuart Anderson at the National Foundation for American Policy found that immigrants were on the founding leadership teams of 24 of the top 50 privately held, venture-backed companies in the US. This is a record number. What is more, Anderson found that in 76% of these companies, immigrants held key positions in engineering, technology or management.

What is the reason for this level of success? Well, consider it from another perspective. American companies are moving some of their executives to posts overseas, in some cases whole regional headquarters. Corporate chieftains, the CEO's and COO's of the world's best companies have recognized that something happens to executives who spend time in countries where the company operates: they gain perspective and knowledge they could never have gotten in their Manhattan office. In this regard, they are no different than college-students on a study year abroad. The young person who returns seems to have received a deeper education than all the rest of their schooling combined.

MIT Sloan Management Review has researched multinational corporations headquartered in the Netherlands, one of the most internationalized economies on earth. What they found in 58 Dutch multinationals participating in the survey found that 57% of those participants had already internationally relocated elements of their headquarters. Further, 67% plan to start or continue relation with in the next five years. Something good happens when workers cross pollinate cultures.

You have to wonder what would have happened to the American car industry in the 1970s and 80s when the Japanese and others were quietly revolutionizing the car industry. They had tons of new ideas, cheaper means of production, greater worker participation and different management thinking and strategy than their American counterparts who were lumbering along. Might a wave of Toyota executives into the office of GM have made a difference?

If it is true that targeting certain sectors of the economy to be filled by appropriately trained and experienced workers could bring vitality and perspective to industry and even to government, then that in turn means a hard look at the supply and demand equation on a sector by sector and industry by industry basis. Broad strokes are neither deliberate nor sufficiently calculating to be effective. Currently, we are trying to fill a tea cup with a fire hose. Predictably there is either no water in the tea cup at all or the tea cup is shattered.

So:

- How many immigrants do we need in the various sectors of our economy?

- How many immigrants do we need to help us with crops and other manual labor?

- How many immigrants do we need to fill engineering jobs and science jobs and medical jobs?

A step in the right direction in fulfilling this kind of strategic plan is BRAIN, Bringing and Retaining Accomplished Innovators for the Nation Act. A new initiative to supplement the current H1-B class of visas, which have proved to be insufficient and has not done enough to fill our resource needs.

Besides targeting workers for jobs in already established industries, new policy initiatives need to go a lot further, and be much more aggressive. For instance, a foreign entrepreneur who decides to immigrate to the United State to start a business with at least five America workers, should be put on a fast track to a Green Card, And by fast, I mean 12 months and not 5 years or even 3 years. Is there any evidence this could be effective. Yes. Nearly 40% of small businesses in five boroughs of New York City were started by immigrants or their children, most of them employing Americans to help grow their business.

Americans from all sides of the political spectrum have long complained about our broken system and the money it takes to run it. We discuss half measures and small steps that by all accounts are unlikely to have any meaningful difference to our economy or society, other than to allow us to pat ourselves on the back for "at least attempting to do something." Our problems are too great to allow for this type of small thinking, and our goals – just like our history – must be grander and bolder. We must turn immigration from a negative, highly-suspect activity into the transforming phenomenon it has been for most of the country's history. Doing away with bureaucratic blockages to immigration, making the process more accessible, affirming that it is good for immigrants to very quickly find their place in the society in which they have chosen to live, become active in their communities and, yes, pay taxes must surely be the way forward.

It is frustrating and hard to explain that with so many experts, sociologists and ordinarily people in agreement about what should be done, that we are not able to make meaningful progress on these issues. Our society is being hijacked by a few who seemingly want to return, as Maureen Dowd has put it, to a "Leave-it-to-Beaverland" that actually never existed, to put immigration reform on hold on hold. I wanted to add my own voice to these others and to support their excellent ideas for repair and reform of our immigration policies and system.

As I have pondered this problem, I have come to the conclusion that none of the proposed solutions go far enough. In spite of my natural inclination to shrink government policies and intervention in business, I have come to realize that in this case, we need a more pro-active government. Because of where we are and what we face, we need more immigration not less, but of a very particular kind. We should be finding ways to keep those people of character and entrepreneurship here. In fact, what I think we should do is seek out immigrants, identify the ones we want, the numbers we need and the skills that we are lacking as a country and then search the world for just such people. This is more than welcome; it is recruitment.

Before I explain this more fully, let me explain the very basic business principal on which I base this somewhat unorthodox idea.

Simply put, when the labor pool does not match up with the economic need, a significant distortion occurs, which is typically accompanied by monetary loss for the business, increased prices for the consumer and ideological debates that rarely lead to real change or progress.

EB-5

Congress has tried to bridge this economic gap, in 1990, with the creation of the EB-5 Visa. This visa allows foreigners who invest at least $500,000 into real estate or a business in the United States (buying stocks or bonds or other indirect investments does not fulfill the requirement) to get a two-year visa for themselves, their spouses and their children. The visas can become Green Cards if the investment produces at least 10 jobs in areas of high unemployment. If the jobs are outside of a "targeted unemployment area," the investment must be $1 million. States set the criteria for high unemployment areas based on specific criteria, such as unemployment at least 150% of the national average.

This process is administered by Regional Centers that determine eligibility based on factors such as what constitutes a "qualified investment" and the direct contribution

And legitimacies of the jobs it purports to generate.

Although the EB-5 program allows for 10,000 immigrants visas a year, only 806 people immigrated in this category in 2007. The rules are tough and require a high-priced lawyer. The bureaucracy is thick with requirements and obstacles, which is the nature of bureaucracy, I suppose, but that's not getting the baby washed.

Andrew Kimball, a real estate investor, is a rather unusual example of how the EB-5 can work to America's advantage. In 2009, Andrew was looking to redevelop the Brooklyn Navy Yard. He is the president of that 300-acre industrial park and when the financial crisis hit, he was unable to retain the $60 million of financing and loans necessary to accomplish the task. So, he boarded a plane to China and ferreted out some potential investors who were intrigued by the idea of investing in America, especially when they heard about the EB-5 offer. Sure, they were rich but until this provision came along, their chances of immigrating to America were laden with all the usual encumbrances of the system. So Kimball returned some time later having secured the $60 million and quite a number of very wealthy potential citizens for the US who will pay taxes here. Based on this investment, the Navy Yard has been able to leverage an additional $81 million from the city and state, creating some 80 jobs in the process.

When you consider how long it takes to get a Green Card, willing investors would find this proposal extremely attractive. And so should the politicians and the country. If someone wants to come to America and invest at least $500,000 and create 10 or more jobs, why would we stop them? In fact, by September 2011, the number of EB-5 applicants ballooned to 3,800 nationally. Wonderful, right? Yes, but the number of applicants is capped, currently, at 10,000. Just as this program has the potential to materially impact our economy, it is likely to be stifled by an artificial policy cap.

If we are ever going to get to the solution of immigration recruitment for strengthening the nations employment needs, we first have to make sure we are not weakening workers and families we already have here.

CHAPTER 9

Making Distinctions, not Exclusions

The average American makes about 3 times as much as the average Mexican – the greatest gap anywhere between neighboring nations. That is why so many of our southern neighbors are crossing the border into the United States. We don't have an immigration problem, we have an inequality problem. Once we recognize that immigration, in particular the right sort, is a 21st century global opportunity for America, not a problem, we will be able to move forward.

Immigration opponents must admit that we cannot, and never will be able to, erect a long enough or high enough fence or have enough guards to keep people out. The French tried that with the Maginot Line, a fortified wall complete with tanks, cannon and thousands of men to keep the Germans out of their country. The Germans went around it. Nor is deportation the answer: it is expensive; it ruins families and does nothing to boost the economy.

No, the solution is to have a smart immigration policy that matches and even recruits those immigrants coming in with the needs of the American economy and work force. This is not as difficult as it sounds.

For a smart immigration system to work, one that consciously pursues immigrants that match our needs, some choices will have to be made. Whenever you think in categories, people automatically suspect exclusion. Perhaps that is inevitable but if we are going to get America working again, we must identify our needs. So here is my rough go at prioritization that will benefit from study and calculation by experts.

I put at the head of the list entrepreneurs who create jobs. This is because it spans the categories of skill sets and socio-economic need. The couple who starts a corner store in a neighborhood that has none and who, as the business grows, employ three, four or even five people, are making a positive impact on their community and on their own financial well-being. The taxes paid by all involved, adds to the nations and cities economic health and the property taxes boost the neighborhood. To put it simply, if you are an entrepreneur and hire five Americans, a Green Card is yours, immediately and for as long as you keep up your end of the deal.

Next are investors, people from all over the world who want to invest in the future of America. We should expand the EB-5 visa program that encourages investment in the United States. If the incentive is not only a good return on their money but also a fast track to a Green Card, I see no problem. The EB-5 program also allows investors to purchase real estate for a minimum of $500,000 and receive a 2 year residency visa for themselves and their immediate family. I also favor expanding the program greatly – our housing market can certainly use the boost. The minimum investment should be dropped to $300,000 and the visa should be granted to 5 years, and the number of visas granted should be raised significantly. The economic impact could be enormous.

Another category suggests itself. We need high-level executives in many industries. So why not import educated, experienced executives that not only can do the job, but who bring a global perspective to the task? I will use myself as an example. My family came to the United States in 1984, as immigrants, as a result of my father's job. My parents and sister have moved back to Germany, but I've stayed on here.. I was able to do so, because in 1984, with corporate sponsorship, getting a Green Card was easy and quick. I'd like to think that I have made a positive contribution to our society. I certainly pay plenty of taxes and support our local merchants.

When it comes to engineers and doctors who have the potential to make several hundred thousand dollars a year, we should welcome them with a Green Card. And so long as they are paying taxes, doing their job, obeying the law, their resident status should continue. Remember, there are nearly 3 ½ million engineering and science based jobs that are currently going unfilled in the United States. If we don't develop a mechanism to fill these jobs with Americans or Immigrants, the employers will figure it out on their own – so far that has meant taking the jobs out of America and moving them to another country. That means a permanent job loss for the U.S.!

As the categories are more precisely identified, we will find job needs in manufacturing, agriculture and many other labor centers. Many of these jobs are tasks that Americans simply don't want to do, but an immigrant with a strong work ethic and a strong back probably does. And if properly matched to a job that needs doing -- Alabama crops for example -- the worker gets a job, the farmer gets his crops picked, the food manufacturer gets their product, the consumer gets the produce and the tax payer at every level gets some relief.

But will it slow the flow of illegal immigrants? Not right away, perhaps, but if the path to citizenship is made, in some cases, automatic and in others simply easier and less expensive, then people will concentrate on those skills and jobs that will land them in the "welcome" category.

The information we need is at our figure tips

The Bureau of Labor Statistics classifies private sector and public sector employment in various divisions and categories—Division A, for example, is agricultural, forestry and fishing. Division B is mining, and so on, including manufacturing. The data identifies how many people, how many Americans are employed in each category and subcategory.

In fact, each month, the Bureau of Labor Statistics collects data on employment, payroll, and paid hours from a sample of establishments. This is important, because it means we have access to ever-changing data, and economists and market analysts have developed very sophisticated models that identify trend lines and project – with a great degree of accuracy – what employment trends will occur over the coming 1, 2, 3 and even 5 years. This means, we have the technology and tools at our fingertips that allows us to adjust our immigration policy as needed. If we construct our immigration policy correctly from the start, to reflect the changes in the need for labor, it will be a great benefit to the US economy and our businesses.

Because the BLS classifies everything by industry, each industry is collected separately and data is broken out to reflect employment hours, earnings, on a statewide, nationwide industry basis.

This information is easily matched up to labor demand and other statistical information that the Bureau of Labor Statistics gathers. Anyone who is interested in taking a look at the depth of the data can just go to http://www.dol.gov or http://www.bls.gov, the Websites for the Department of Labor, and the Bureau of Labor Statistics respectively. Combined, these sites are an enormous source of information that is broken down by geography, by industry, by occupation, productivity, wages, earnings, and benefits, all of which is right at our fingertips. Wall Street uses it, our politicians should too. The government reports the information but in terms of immigration, does not use it to improve the economy, at least not sufficiently. It is not being used aggressively to develop immigration policies that match up supply and demand.

Given the significant advances in technology, response rates and thereby flexibility in establishing policy, we can move out of the 1950's style policy implementation into the 21st century. *[Ft.note: Employment data refers to persons on established payrolls who receive pay for any part of the pay period that includes the 12th day of the month. In other words: You have to work at least 12 days out of the month to be counted. So, it eliminates the labor pool requirements for part-time jobs or minimal work.]*

Take, for example, the construction industry: construction employees include employees in the construction sector, working supervisors, qualified craft employees, mechanics, apprentices, helpers, laborers and so forth. They are all engaged in new work, alteration, demolition, repair, maintenance, and the like. Again, we have very clear data that shows what is being built, how much is planning to be built, how many people are currently in there.

The point is that we can pretty accurately adjust the number of individuals that we allow in under work permits per classification. I recognize that it is a fairly radical proposal, because we are talking about treating America and our immigration policy like a business. I realize that countries are not businesses because they have a responsibility to citizens beyond a return on investment. But a country can be compared, I think, to a charitable trust, which has a wider mandate than profit, but still must use business principles to satisfy its constituency's goals.

I know that there are people who will be uneasy with applying business principles to the economy because in their minds businesses and corporations are at best suspect, even though they generate much of the money (given a sensible tax code) that runs the country. But I found the point made by Dr. Robert Shiller of Yale University compelling in a recent speech concerning the earthquake in Haiti which cost tens of thousands of people their lives. In the 1990s there was a quake of similar size and strength in San Francisco: six people, regrettably, died. What made the difference? Well, part of the answer has to do with a deeper infrastructure in San Francisco. But another big part of the answer is enforced building codes. In Haiti, there are none because there are no insurance companies to insist on them.

In fact, I put down my own well-being as a homeowner to my insurance company, Chubb, which insists on fire extinguishers, fire alarms and smoke detectors, proper wiring, even a strong foundation. I get a lot more for my premium than an assurance that if against all odds, the place burns down. I get daily peace of mind knowing that my primary home environment conforms to a known standard.

Fear versus the Future

What can be the result of a sensible immigration policy? Are we to fear the influx of foreign-born people? To answer that, consider New York City.

In the five boroughs of New York, foreign-born residents make up 37 percent of the population. That includes 50% of the doctors in New York City, 33% of financial managers and 25% of architects. In fact, New York City would have lost population in the past several decades without immigration.

Their presence has revitalized neighborhoods, meant thousands of new, small businesses and rehabilitated the housing stock. Without immigrants buying up multi-family housing units the housing market would be in far worse shape than it is today.

It is generally true that immigrants are attracted to large cities where they find people of like background in terms of culture and traditions. There is, however, at least one upstate mayor, Albert Jurczynski of Schenectady, who bucked this trend. He went all out to attract Guyanese living in Richmond Hills, Queens to move to his city. He offered free bus trips to visit the city and put out welcome mats to members of the community. He succeeded in doubling his foreign-born population and reversed a 50 year decline in the city's population. His new residents included many industrious entrepreneurs who are bringing new wealth and economic health to a city once in decline.

Moreover, immigrants are fitting in. Miriam Jordan recently wrote an article in the Wall Street Journal where she found some 80% of immigrants living above the poverty line, not the common impression. About 70% are completing high school and 55% are fully engaged in the American dream by owning their own home.

Hispanics sometimes seem to get the brunt of criticism about immigration but the figures show that 75% of them are above the poverty line, 58% or so have completed high school and home ownership is at about 40% but rising. Yes, the naturalization rate is lower for this group, but over half of them speak English well. This figure will continue to rise as their children become fully engaged in our educational system.

Okay, assimilation is on a positive track and the longer immigrants are here the better they fit in. But how do we get them to not only assimilate but to be much more productive members of our society. We do that by matching skill sets to labor pools.

Matching up labor pools with labor demand is essential. But it is not enough long-term. Programs such as the California Dream Act, the same sort of provision was passed in Ohio -- are critical because they allow for a greater sense of integration into society. The other long-term aspect of the immigration solution is education. We know that education is the key to finding better paying jobs but our system is not producing enough doctors, mathematicians and physicists to fill the demand. Immigrants can and need to be part of the solution.

As we pointed out before, immigrants are not just workers, they are consumers. And they want more than anything a chance to be in America, to work and to build a better life for their children- just like your grandfather and grandmother did, wherever they came from.

One of the mistakes in having an exclusionary immigration policy is the lost opportunity for a different way of thinking about the world. As long as we have a model that has the view that immigrants are ignorant and a pull on services, that is the result we will get. But if are able to retain educated people from around the world and educate the ones who are here, whole new worlds of thinking can open to us.

As much as we like to all imagine a world with strict borders, the reality is that the real world is much more fluid. Technology has greatly affected everything we do, including the way we do business, of course, and how we need to look at immigration.

Take, for example, Doctors Malvinder and Shivinder Singh, brothers who built Fortis Hospitals in India. Both were educated in the United States with the result that they articulate a helpful viewpoint: They say, "If you live only in India, you naturally measure yourself against Indian standards. If you have lived abroad, you measure yourself against the best of the world."

The result for their hospitals is that they have incorporated some of the best things that India has to offer and some of the best things that the U.S. has to offer in terms of style of medicine. Fortis Hospitals re-imagined the American excellence and fit it to a frugal Indian setting. Whereas a leading surgeon in America might perform 250 to 350 operations a year, a surgeon in India at Fortis Hospital will perform 1200 surgeries a year. The reason they are able to do that is because the surgeon in India has a large, large number of helpers, nurses and non-nurses, to take care of all the mundane tasks leaving surgeons free to concentrate on their expertise. Doctors at Fortis Hospital are very well paid. They earn almost the as much as their U.S. counterparts. But as a result of the efficiencies, a kidney operation that might cost 100,000 dollars in the United States will cost less than 10,000 dollars at Fortis Hospital in India. Could their style of doing medicine have an impact on American healthcare costs? Perhaps – But without the perspective of people like the Singhs we may find ourselves continuing to do things the way we have always done them when there are clearly other, more efficient models out there.

Because migrants see the world through more than one cultural lens, they can spot opportunities and ways to improve the process much quicker than somebody who has only had a single cultural experience in their life.

For example, Cheung Yan, a Chinese woman living here in America, noticed that Americans threw out mountains of waste paper. So? So she realized that the ships that bring all those "Made in China" articles to the U.S. often steam back to China empty. And? So what she did is gather tons of that waste paper and shipped it to China on otherwise empty ships for recycling into cardboard boxes many of which are then returned to America with televisions inside. Mrs. Cheung is now a billionaire. Why didn't an American spot that opportunity? Because her cultural lens was different from ours! She made a connection that anyone might have made but nobody did until she added two and two together, became wealthy, and more importantly (from an economic perspective), now has nearly 10,000 employees – all newly created jobs as a result of her perspective and ingenuity. The world is full of budding young Cheung Yans and we are foolish not to encourage them more.

Immigrants are only one-eighth of America's population. But a quarter of the engineering and technology firms started between 1995 and 2005 had an immigrant founder, according to a study from Vivek Wadwha at Duke University. The exceptional creativity of immigrants is a reflection of their desire to move up on the social and economic ladder and not taking anything for granted.

To support this thesis, Northwestern University researchers conducted a series of experiments during which they compared MBA students who lived abroad with otherwise similar students who had not lived abroad. The experiment involved giving each candidate a candle, a box of matches and a box of drawing pins. The student's task was to attach the candle to a wall so that it burned properly and did not drip wax on the table or the floor. This Duncker candle problem, as it is known, is considered a good test of creativity because it requires you to imagine something being used for a purpose quite different from its usual one. (Before reading on, can you successfully complete this task?)

Nearly 60-percent of migrants saw the solution, while only 42% of their American counter parts where able to come up with the answer in the required time. (By the way, when this or similar tests are administered in other nations, similar results are achieved

– the people with a more diverse cultural background perform significantly better). The answer: pinning the drawing pin box to the wall as a makeshift sconce. The creativity of immigrants and migrants is enhanced by their ability to enroll collaborators both far off and nearby. For example, in Silicon Valley, more than half of Chinese and Indian scientists and engineers share tips about technology or business opportunities with people in their home countries, according to AnnaLee Saxenian of the University of California at Berkley.

Further, a study by the Kauffman Foundation, a think tank, found that 84% of returning Indian entrepreneurs maintains at least monthly contact with family and friends in America and 66% are in contact at least that often with former colleagues. For entrepreneurs who return to China, the figures are 81% and 55% respectively.

Rugged individualism in America is one way to succeed, but it may not be the only way. Just as ethnic communities stuck together in former times, even while they were being assimilated, so many immigrants today have a deep social network for support. In fact, with the amazing and growing technology of the Internet, we are all learning the interconnectedness of social -- and business -- interaction. Borders may be helpful for maps, but they are increasingly irrelevant to economic reality, where business seeps, migrates and wanders across borders with little thought to passports. People themselves seem to have thrown out their maps as well.

One great example of where this borderless business landscape is already operational in China. China is, of course, enormous. More Chinese people live outside mainland China than French people live in France. You can find Chinese and in most cases Chinatowns in certainly every country around the globe and virtually in every major city around the globe. Another example is the some 22 million ethnic Indians scattered across every continent and living outside of India. Lebanese people are working and living in West Africa and Latin America, Japanese in Brazil and Peru. The list could multiply because there is practically no reason for people to stay where they were born if they don't want to. And if they have wanderlust, a destination is only a few clicks away.

Until the mid-twentieth century, it was relatively difficult to stay in touch with your family and loved ones once you immigrated somewhere. Flights or travel were expensive and long. The Internet and telephone calls were nonexistent in many places. In particular, coming to the United States, which everyone knows has a high standard of living and has the reputation for opportunity, was a tough choice to make because it would mean leaving your home land behind, more or less, for good. A century ago, a migrant boarding a ship to sail to America and would never see his friends or families again. Today, thanks to cheap flights and instant communication, people can stay in touch with the places they came from. Today, an immigrant can text his mother and call his brother and wire money in minutes. All of this means that immigration is not so difficult an emotional choice as it once was but the same motivation that has brought most immigrants to America -- the quest for a better life -- is still the driving force. You might think that this ability to keep in touch with their native culture would slow assimilation. No study, however, indicates that that is the case. Far from wanting to change the American cultural landscape, most immigrants are proving they want to be part of it.

We have identified that one of the main reasons the immigrant population pays less in taxes than the average American or their American counterpart is not as a result of being paid less than Americans, but rather because many work in low skill, low wage jobs. (One could easily argue that illegal immigrants pay more than their share in taxes, as they cannot participate in most social services, and are never eligible to any form of tax refund) Although it is true that first-generation immigrants are not well educated, second and third generation immigrants continuously typically improve their education levels. It is still true that anyone, including immigrants, who gets a broader level of education and has the drive to succeed, has more opportunities to do so in America than anywhere else in the world. We should be proud of this, and we should continue to encourage this level of entrepreneurship.

It is not enough to simply view or think about immigrants as those who do low level work in fields. Sure, that work will continue for a long time and we will probably need unskilled labor into the future. But if we get stuck with that model, we will do ourselves no favors. An immigration policy of stability, education, assimilation and upward mobility is critical if we are going to reverse our declining competitiveness with China, India and Brazil. It will not happen without some fundamental changes in the way we treat immigrants. The expensive and counterproductive policy of hounding individuals, splitting families, denying educational opportunities for second generation immigrants and turning out of the country highly educated ones is getting us nowhere. It is time to throw out the ideas that are not producing the results we want, and embrace the ones that will make us stronger and more prosperous.

Here are some thoughts on what politically and administratively needs to occur to start fixing the problem. They are in part based on some of the work the Partnership for a New American Economy, has done. The organization, which was created by Mayor Michael Bloomberg, is a bipartisan economic think tank made up of business leaders such as Stephen Ballmer, CEO of Microsoft, Ursula Burns, Chairman and CEO of Xerox Corporation, Rupert Murdoch, a naturalized American Citizens. (www.renewoureconomy.org)

1. Catalogue our needs, both current and expected based on data we already have.

2. Determine how many "different" immigrants we need to meet our needs.

3. Empower the INS to review all current visa applicants to reduce the existing backlog and match up the current talent pool with our labor needs.

4. Develop policies that reward and incentivize people, immigrant or not, to become entrepreneurs and create more jobs.

5. Recognize that each state in the Union has varying needs and allow flexibility on a state by state basis to adjust the number of immigrants needed.

6. Do not fall into the trap of protectionism. Being patriotic and wanting what is best for America requires courage and foresight, not shortsightedness and pandering.

As we grow in the realization that immigrants and immigration can greatly benefit the United States, we need to move our current set of policies (which is often ideology dressed up as policy) from a family and country based system to an employment based system. Specifically, we need to let the economy and business need set the levels of desired immigration.

To get started, we need to empower the INS to clear all naturalization backlogs. We need to process the paperwork of those waiting to become U.S. citizens or to enter the country legally at a much quicker pace. Let me reiterate that we should arrest and deport illegal immigrants who are violent criminals and felons keeping in mind that is a very small percentage of the immigrant population and there is no proven link that more immigration leads to higher levels of crime. To the contrary, empirical evidence suggests that illegal immigrants have very low crime rates, for fear of being caught and deported. Focusing on deporting criminals is the stated policy of the Obama administration, but judging by the number of non-criminals who are detained and deported, the policy has a lot of holes or a lack of will.

Furthermore, we should require that all of our embassies around the world work with local governments to facilitate and incentivize graduates from elite foreign universities who graduate with engineering, mathematics and science degrees to immigrate to the United States. We need this talent pool, and we should aggressively pursue it, just as other nations are pursuing our talented graduates.

We need to review the procedures for handing out H1B Visas and L1 visas and greatly increase the number of people that receive those visas, in particular to marry the job and labor demand with the labor supply. We need to recognize that some 25% of businesses started in our country are started by immigrants and in some cases are started by students who are here and remain in the country despite being technically illegal. Do we really want to deport these entrepreneurs, the very people that we need and who are going to create jobs in the United States? I propose that the answer to that is an absolute and categorical, no.

We also need to work on an international solution, recognizing that immigration and migration are natural to us as human beings and so there needs to be an international solution and not just with Mexico or Canada but around the globe. That means that we need a broad immigration plan that has the centerpiece of education as well as a mechanism to turn every immigrant in the country into a taxpayer and to truly become integrated into our society.

If we were to come up with a workable amnesty program as some have suggested, the flipside of that would mean that we would need much stricter enforcement and much harsher rules for deportation—not detention—of people who break significant laws. Most importantly, this process would need to be deliberate and require extra effort on behalf of those applying for amnesty. One suggested solution is to allow the current population of illegals to remain in the United States under a special visa. They would be required to pay taxes, remain employed, and obey all of our laws. Any infarction other than a minor traffic violation would lead to immediate and irreversible expulsion. In other words, if we give somebody amnesty to remain in the United States and they break a law, then deportation is the automatic penalty without exception. There needs to be harsh consequences for breaking the rules.

We need to recognize that this is an opportunity and that we need to control the flow of immigration in a much more economically beneficial way and that includes fining and taxing corporations who purposely hire illegal immigrants. I do not necessarily mean the local sandwich shop that has the busboy in the back, although that probably needs to be addressed as well. I am talking about large corporations who purposely hire illegal immigrants and pay them sub-par wages. There has been plenty of cases from home builders to shopping centers and everything in between that are doing business that way.

I think that a college graduate with an engineering degree or a mathematics or science degree should get an instant green card, at least as long as we need to have the jobs filled in the United States. Let us do anything and everything we can to create greater revenues, increase our tax revenues and improve our overall countries fiscal and economic health. Part of achieving that is to recognize the unwavering truth that legalizing immigration and changing our immigration policy will pump billions of dollars into our economy.

America has a long history of taking bold steps and being courageous in its decision making process. Today, as our economy faces staggering debt levels and rising deficits, we need to rekindle that fire. America must once again make aggressive, revolutionary policy decisions to solve its problems. We need to develop a long-term policy for immigration, education and our social programs. Not too long ago, in 2003, Congress developed a forward thinking set of immigration policies that was widely supported by Democrats and Republicans. President Bush endorsed the bill, which was sponsored by Republican Senator John McCain and Democratic Senator Ted Kennedy. Unfortunately for all of us, the fringes – the far right and far left of each party hated the bill and succeeded in defeating it. In what, for many, marked the birth of fringe politics, the bill never even came to a vote. The radical right wing of the Republican Party opposed any provision that provided a path to citizenship or permanent residency, while the ultra-liberal left of the Democratic Party fought against the components of the legislation that shifted immigration to be skills based, and the unions objected to the temporary workers permits. The fact that the extremes of each party hated the bill should have been plenty of evidence that it was a great piece of legislation.

America has been a leader in the world in so many ways, is a vital and vibrant country with a strong history of immigration and tremendous ability to assimilate various groups. Over the past few years, in part in response to the recession and high unemployment rate, we have allowed our policies and rhetoric to be driven by the extremes of our respective political parties. Unfortunately, if we let these factions continue to drive the discussion, we will all lose. America is a wonderful country that has tremendous resources and we remain the place the world looks to for guidance and leadership. We must continue to foster the spirit that has made America great to ensure we remain great.

A short personal story written by my friend and contributor to this book:

If you are anything like me, after a hard weeks' work, nothing is more pleasant than joining a couple of friends and your spouse at your favorite local restaurant. After all, who doesn't enjoy a fine meal, a few laughs and great service? One of the reasons it is all so pleasant is the level of service, not just from the wait staff, but also from the support staff of cooks, bus boys, dishwashers and the welcome deliverer of a replacement fork. Glasses appear on shelves from someplace in the "back" sometimes in spectacular fashion: the other day, we witnessed a bus boy holding 32 large wine glasses in one hand while with the other hand he deftly plucked them from their precariously and placed them safely on a high shelf.

Many of these people who do this support staff work are illegal immigrants. We all know that, but sometimes we like to pretend we don't. There are 11 to 12 million illegal immigrants in this country and the nation spends some 5 billion dollars every year trying to get rid of them (according to Kumar Kibble, deputy director of Immigrations Customs and Enforcement). It's not that illegals wouldn't like to become legal but once here as an illegal alien, there is no path to a green card or citizenship. The reason there are so many of them in every single restaurant in Fairfield and Fairfield County is that virtually no American will take these jobs and no restaurant can afford to be without them. (There are about 18,500 illegal immigrants working in Connecticut, about 4.5% of the work force). It's not that the restaurateurs are trying to save money by using illegal immigrants -- they are paid relatively well -- it is, as one owner told us, "simply a matter of labor supply. Without these people we couldn't exist."

Some opine (even while being served at the restaurant): "But they don't pay taxes -- they should be grateful to be here." They are grateful because without these jobs, their families back in their country of origin would have a much harder time than they already do. As for taxes, no doubt some illegals don't pay, but the ones in restaurants do -- Federal tax, State tax, Medicare tax, Social Security tax and unemployment insurance tax. If all unauthorized immigrants were removed from Connecticut, the state would lose $5.6 billion in economic activity, $2.5 billion in gross state product, and approximately 24,119 jobs, even accounting for adequate market adjustment time, according to a report by the Perryman Group, which tracks immigrant activity. Unauthorized immigrants in Connecticut paid $120.5 million in state and local taxes in 2010, according to data from the Institute for Taxation and Economic Policy. That number includes $14.3 million in state income taxes, $31.2 million in property taxes and $75 million in sales taxes.

What they don't get in return is a social security card, social security benefits or unemployment payments if they lose their jobs. Few have any health insurance and contrary to popular myth, emergency rooms demand payment.

Meet Pablo, an illegal immigrant from Ecuador (not his real name), who works in one of Fairfield's best restaurants. When he came to this country he was 16. He agreed to talk to Fairfield Magazine, a somewhat bold decision since if he is identified, he could be deported, the ever-present dread threat all illegals live with.

Now 18, his manner is shy and serious, though occasionally you can get him to grant a warm smile. For the most part, people have been kind to him -- a bartender at the restaurant took up a collection among patrons for a Christmas gift.

"I left my mother in the town where we lived. My father, a cousin and an uncle had left before me. To make the journey, the charge was $12,000, which my mother gave to me. You have to pay at every stage." The idea is to make contact with an "enterprise," for want of a better term, that knows the ropes. In Pablo's case he was part of a group of 25 ("all kinds," he says, "men, pregnant women, children, young, old.") They are taken by plane to, say, Honduras, thence to Mexico and eventually up to the U.S. border. Many of them swim the Rio Grande. "They feed us yes, but it is not good food." Once at the border they follow a "man who knows the way" into the Arizona desert. Once, the guide, sensing ICE agents were coming, ordered them all to scatter. Pablo found a good hiding spot behind a rock but others were not so lucky. Only 5 of the initial 25 made it out of the desert -- the rest were captured and jailed. Of course, they didn't get their money back. "After this, those of us who were left still had a three day walk through the desert. No food. But the big problem was no water."

The next stage took Pablo to Los Angeles (others go to Houston or other cities) where the newcomers shelter in a crowded house with other travelers. "Here you make the final payment. $8,000. If you don't, they take you back." Pablo traveled cross-country in a van with as many as the vehicle could hold to Connecticut, where his father and cousin lived. But his father had "married" an American woman (without ending his Guatemalan marriage) and no longer wanted anything to do with his son. For a while Pablo lived with his cousin in Bridgeport, but now has a room with an elderly couple there.

He's worked at various restaurants but currently, through a friend who could vouch for his honesty, he works as a bus boy here in Fairfield. He goes to school by day and works from 4 o'clock until closing at the restaurant. He sends about a quarter of his earnings back to Ecuador and lives on the rest. He has a car but no driver's license because he doesn't have a social security number. He's never been stopped but "I am very afraid that one day it will happen. They might send me back."

Pablo will graduate from a Bridgeport High School this year and would like to go to college but that seems too fantastic a dream at the moment (again no Social Security number). Just being here is enough for now.

Another Illegal we talked to, we'll call him Juan, had a similar story. His wife is with him but his 7-year old daughter who he has not seen in 5 years is back home with a grandmother. He drives the car of his brother-in-law who was stopped at a toll plaza and failing to show a driver's license, was jailed for three months and then deported. He was lucky because his relatives here came up with the $1600 for the unrestricted plane ticket the ICE requires deportees to buy. Otherwise, he would have been jailed longer. His wife and children are still here.

Juan works four double shifts (10:30 am until closing) four of the six days he works. His earnings pay his mortgage in Ecuador and for the support of his daughter. The rest goes to rent, gas, food -- the usual stuff. He is glad for the job since it pays about twice what he could make back home and may stay another five years if is unable to somehow get his daughter here. Otherwise, he'll go back sooner, and with his departure we will lose just a little bit more of the American Dream and what makes America so great.

Daniel England is a freelance writer and occasional speaker on matters theological. He was the former speechwriter for the Speaker of the New Jersey Assembly and also for the CEO of Texaco and President of Texaco Europe. He served as managing editor for an award winning publication, Agenda, that won best business magazine three years running in the U.K. Daniel is holds three masters degrees including an M.A. (in theology) from Cambridge University in England.

Index of People:

Index of Companies:

Index of Terms:

Congressional Acts:

Institutes and Institutions:

Sources and acknowledgements:

CNBC.com, August 2012 – Mark Koba senior editor
Michael Wildes, Immigration Attorney, Wildes & Weinberg
The Economist – September 1, 2012 US edition.
The Wall Street Journal – September 14, 2012 Online Edition / Patrick Barta, Wilawan Watcharasakwet, Vibhuti Agarwal = The Rise of the Underground
The International Monetary Fund: Hiding in the Shadows, March 2002

AlterNet – Sarah Jaffe: Inside the Trillion-Dollar Undergroung Economy Keeping Many Americans (Barely) Afloat in Desperate Times: September 16, 2011
AlterNet.org; Sarah Jaffe,

Center for American Progress – Immigration Policy Center
Raising the Floor for American Workers, Dr. Raul Hinojosa-Ojeda - January 2010

U.S. Department of Homeland Security – Budgets for fiscal years 2003 through 2010

United Nations Department of Economic and Social Affairs "World Population Prospects: 2008 edition"

Cato Institute 2009 report "Restriction or Legalization: Measuring the Economic Benefit of Immigration Reform" (Washington: Cato Institute 2009)

Rajeev Goyle and David A. Jaeger, "Deporting the Undocumented: A Cost Assessment"

Congressional Budget Office – The Budget and Economic Outlook: Fiscal Years 2009 to 2019" (2009)

White House Report "Immigration's Economic Impact" – June 20, 2007

G. Ottaviano and G. Peri "Rethinking the Effects of Immigration on Wages" 2006

National Academy Press 1997

G. Borjas – Heaven's Door: Immigration Policy and the American Economy, Princeton: Princeton University Press, 1999

D. Card – Is the New Immigration Really so Bad? NBER Working Paper 11547

Council of Economic Advisor, Economic Report of the President, Washington DC: US Gov Printing Office 2005

J. Passel – "The Size and Characteristics of the Unauthorized Migrant Population in the U.S." Pew Hispanic Center, 2006

U.S. Census Bureau, Statistical Abstract of the United States: 2012

Chronicle Magazine (Chroniclemagazine.org) – May 11, 2005 – The Economic Impact of Immigration: Paying for the Privilege – Peter Brimelow, May 11 2009 edition

Business Insider – Impact of Mexican Immigrant on U.S. Economy

The Brookings Institute: The Hamilton Project – Michael Greenstone and Adam Looney September 2010

University of California, Davis – Giovanni Peri: The Migration Policy Institute 2010: The Impact of Immigrants in Recession and Economic Expansion

SOURCES AND ACKNOWLEDGEMENTS:

Pew Research Center – Social & Demographic Trends, February 11, 2009

Jeffrey S. Passel and D'Vera Cohn for the Pew Research Center, Washington DC

The Board of Trustees, Federal Old-Age and survivors insurance and Federal Disability Insurance Trust Funds – The 2012 annual report of the board of trustees of the federal old-age and survivors insurance and federal disability insurance trust funds: April 23, 2012

The Wall Street Journal: A GOP Opportunity on Immigration, Jon Huntsman

Crains: New York Business: Dreamers, businesses cheer as deferred action clocks in – Daniel Massey

Connecticut Post: July 2012 – Looking abroad to fill job positions by Robert Miller

The New York Times, Saturday August 4, 2012 – Young Immigrants can file to defer deportation by Julia Preston

The New York Times, Sunday August 5, 2012 – An American Model for attracting Tech Jobs: By Bill Vlasic, Hiroko Tabuchi, Charles Duhigg

The Economist US Edition – August 11, 2012 Virility symbols: American fertility is now lower than that of France

The Wall Street Journal – Monday November 14, 2011: Immigrants are still fitting in, by Miriam Jordan

About the author:

Oliver Pursche is the President of GGFS and the co-portfolio manager of the GMG Defensive Beta Fund (MPDAX). Mr. Pursche is a tri-lingual financial executive who grew up in Europe. He has a strong academic and business back ground, combining his 20 years of experience working for venerable firms like PaineWebber and Neuberger Berman with classroom knowledge he garnered taking graduate level courses at the University of Pennsylvania's Wharton School of Business, and holding an undergraduate degree from Bentley University. This combination of knowledge and international perspective, along with his sales, marketing, sales management and global asset management experience is critical when making business decisions in a world that is increasingly impacted by global affairs. Mr. Pursche is a thought leader in the investment community, writing weekly investment columns for The Wall Street Journal online, Forbes.com, TheStreet.com and as a frequent guest on Bloomberg Television, Fox Business News, CNBC as well as other national business media outlets.

Made in the USA
Charleston, SC
16 February 2013